Celebrate
SUNDAY

Celebrate
SUNDAY

52 IDEAS TO HELP
YOUR FAMILY DELIGHT
IN THE SABBATH

LANI OLSEN HILTON

Covenant Communications, Inc.

This book is dedicated to my parents, Maynard and Sally Olsen,
who I love dearly and who instilled in me a love for the holy Sabbath

Cover image: Bunting Flags © Makkuro_GL, courtesy istockphoto.com

Cover design copyright © 2017 by Covenant Communications, Inc.

Published by Covenant Communications, Inc.
American Fork, Utah

Printed in the United States of America
First Printing: September 2017

22 21 20 19 18 17   10 9 8 7 6 5 4 3 2 1

ISBN 978-1-52440-187-0

Given the direction from the Brethren to make the Sabbath more meaningful, *Celebrate Sunday: Fifty-Two Ideas to Help Your Children Delight in the Sabbath* offers fresh insights for ways families can find joy in this holy day. Each chapter covers one idea that parents or another family member can easily implement, most of them within 5 minutes.

This book is for busy parents who want appropriate, practical, and fun ideas at their fingertips. Looking for a gospel game? Try "Apples to Chapels" or "Scripture Scrabble." Want to make your Sabbath a little more gospel-oriented? Browse the chapter "Explore the Sources" or "Power from Prophets." These ideas—which include the themes of meaningful celebrations, field trips, engaging family history ideas, and much more—will help parents involve their children in enjoyable, meaningful Sabbath gatherings.

9

TABLE OF CONTENTS

Introduction 1

Family Home Evening Lesson:
The Doctrine of the Holy Sabbath 9

Part 1: Gospel Games 13

   1. Scripture Land 15

   2. Reverse Gospel Pictionary 17

   3. Chutes and Ladders—Scripture Style 19

   4. Sunday Charades 23

   5. Apples to Chapels 25

   6. Gospel 20 Questions 27

   7. Bible Balderdash 29

   8. Scripture Bingo 31

   9. Scripture Scrabble 33

   10. Where in the World Is Deborah? 35

   11. The Magic Sunday Square 37

   12. Scripture Sports: Scripture Basketball and
       Scripture Golf 41

   13. Conference Jeopardy 43

Part 2: Significant Dates/Anniversary Celebrations 45

   14. Love Legacy—February 47

15. The Publication of the Book of Mormon—
    March 26, 1830 49

16. The Return of Elijah—April 3, 1836 51

17. The Birthday of the Church—April 6 53

18. Sundays Preceding Easter, Palm Sunday,
    & Easter Sunday—March/April 55

19. The Seven Sundays Following Easter—April/May 57

20. The Restoration of the Priesthood—May 15, 1829 61

21. The Organization of the Primary—August 25, 1878 63

22. The Appearance of Angel Moroni and Joseph
    Obtaining the Golden Plates—Sept 21–22, 1823 65

23. The Family: A Proclamation to the World—
    September 23, 1995 67

24. Conference Celebrations—
    First Weekends in April and October 69

25. Joseph Smith's Birthday—December 23, 1805 71

Part 3: Family History Snowballing 73

26. Indexing Races 75

27. Family History Quiz Creations 77

28. Sharing Mission Records 79

29. Joy in Past Journeys 81

30. Focus on Faces 83

31. Ancestor Anniversaries and Birthdays 85

32. Grandparent Guesstures 87

33. When I Was Young 89

34. Family History Live Recordings 91

35. Jump to Journaling 93

Part 4: Gospel Study 95

36. Explore the Sources 97

37. Presenting *Preach My Gospel* 99

38. Miraculous Music 103

39. Progress with Programs 105

40. Reporting Live from *For the Strength of Youth* 107

41. Amazing Memorizing... 109

42. Gospel Art 111

43. Power from Prophets... 113

44. Stories of Jesus 115

45. Family Council without the Family Feud 117

46. Individual Interviews 121

Part 5: Special Guests and Field Trips 123

47. Returned Missionary Guests 125

48. Wisdom from Near and Far 127

49. Plan of Salvation Field Trips.................................. 129

50. I Love to See the Temple 131

51. Visit the Widows and Fatherless............................... 133

52. Sunday Service 135

Conclusion.. 137

Appendix A: Activities by Age 139

Appendix B: A System for Your Sabbath............................. 143

INTRODUCTION

A MOTHER WAS SADDENED WHEN her young son angrily expressed that he hated Sunday because he was not allowed to do anything! She realized that Sunday in their home had become a day of saying, "Don't!" Does this sound familiar? If we are always on the defensive telling our children all the things they cannot do on Sunday, we may miss valuable opportunities to help them engage in meaningful activities. What can we do so our children will look forward to Sunday? How can we make Sunday a day that is a delight for our children and still have it be a day of worship?

Elder Tad R. Callister taught: "Parents . . . are to be the prime gospel teachers and examples for our children—not the bishop, the Sunday School, the Young Women or Young Men, but the parents. . . . We might all ask ourselves: do our children receive our best spiritual, intellectual, and creative efforts, or do they receive our leftover time and talents, after we have given our all to our Church calling or professional pursuits?" ("Parents: The Prime Gospel Teachers of Their Children," *Ensign*, November 2014).

Quotes like this have helped me realize I need to put my "best spiritual, intellectual, and creative efforts" into making Sabbath worship in our home worthwhile and productive. Recent Church meetings have re-emphasized a letter from the First Presidency stating, "We counsel parents and children to give highest priority to family prayer, family home evening, gospel study and instruction, and wholesome family activities. However worthy and appropriate other demands or activities may be, they must not be permitted to displace the divinely-appointed duties that only parents and families can adequately perform" ("Letter from the First Presidency," February 11, 1999).

Even though our family has daily family scripture study and prayer, and weekly family home evening, I have learned that some of the best "gospel study and instruction" as referred to in the letter from the First Presidency can happen on Sunday. My family delights in the Sabbath as we engage in activities that help us learn the gospel and enjoy together time that invites the Spirit into our home. When we push aside less-essential tasks, we find ample time for deliberate learning activities.

The Sabbath is a holy day and how we treat it sends a sign to the Lord (see Ezekiel 20:20). However, energetic children of differing ages can pose the greatest challenge to keeping the Sabbath a holy day. Besides being too tired or distracted, one of the most common obstacles we face is lacking the know-how to engage our children in gospel-centered learning.

About This Book

The ideas presented in this book do not require extensive gospel knowledge, fancy materials, or lesson preparation time. They are ideal for those who desire a variety of appropriate Sabbath activities at their fingertips. Each chapter includes one simple activity to do on a Sunday before or after church. These activities are meant to unify family members, facilitate gospel learning, and invite the Spirit of the Lord. Sunday can be a day the whole family draws closer to each other and to the Savior.

Let's be clear. This book is *not* a to-do list for already overburdened parents. It is *not* another program that families need to do or feel guilty about not doing. It is *not* something that will be appropriate for every stage of life. Finally, it is *not* the sum of all possible ideas for delighting in the Sabbath.

This book *is* a collection of 52 easy-to-implement ideas that will be a good start to help your family look forward to this sanctified day. It *is* a resource with tips to help you simply teach children in meaningful and creative ways. It *is* full of practical ideas that can bless your family and help you design your Sabbath day. I hope you will adapt and tweak these ideas as you make them your own. I hope you will experience how easy it can be to immerse your family in the scriptures. I hope you will find joy in bringing appropriate fun into the day. Fostering family unity and encouraging learning will both invite the Spirit of the Lord. The possibilities of spiritually strengthening activities are endless. Children can look forward to the Sabbath in your home. I know firsthand that the Sabbath day can truly be a delight, even (and especially!) with a busy family!

Set Yourself Up for Success

Over the past fifteen years I have *gradually* incorporated the games, celebrations, and other experiences described in this book. Flexibility has been foremost! Frequently, I modify the chosen activity dramatically and do only the essential aspect of it. Realistically, this can mean spending 3–5 minutes on something I would have preferred to spend 20 minutes on. Please don't feel like you must experience instant success or do every activity presented precisely as described in order to properly teach or invite the Spirit, or for the Sabbath to be a delight!

When I have shared some of these ideas in firesides or conversations, sometimes listeners appear overwhelmed. Some might declare with exasperation that it is too hard to go from doing nothing to doing ALL these activities. You certainly don't need to follow the suggestions below in order to feel successful, but they may be helpful as you begin.

Start with Low Expectations. Be realistic. Just like with family home evening or family scripture study, you may experience chaos. Even with the best of intentions, sometimes things get messy and kids get cranky. Don't give up! We can press forward and continue making an effort to have meaningful Sabbath activities even when previous attempts may have failed miserably. As Elder David A. Bednar taught: "No one event may appear to be very impressive or memorable. But just as the . . . strokes of paint complement each other and produce an impressive masterpiece, so our consistency in doing seemingly small things can lead to significant spiritual results" ("More Diligent and Concerned at Home," *Ensign*, November 2009). I know this is true. Only the adversary wants us to get discouraged and think our efforts are worthless.

Simple Rewards Can Motivate. It is hard to believe our efforts are doing any good when contention and crankiness pervade the room or children refuse to participate. While we don't want to encourage a family culture where we cannot do anything good without receiving a reward, sometimes a little external motivation can be helpful. This is especially true when just starting or getting back into a habit. For example, a small piece of gum given to the family members who are ready when called goes a long way. Even offering one chocolate chip, mint, or other tiny treat for every letter written, pair of lines memorized, or article read and reported on can make all the difference between compliance and complaining.

Keep in mind that the wise keep the rewards small. Filling bodies with too many treats can start working against you. Rewards can also be non-edible, like a coupon for a day without chores or a trip to the park on another day of the week.

Try a Power Hour. Investing just an hour doing a few of these activities can change what Sunday offers your family. You may call it a Power Hour. If an hour sounds overwhelming, try a Power Half-Hour! I don't suggest that you spend a whole day studying *Preach My Gospel* or singing hymns (see chapters 37 and 38), but a few minutes of studying and uplifting music, combined with some gospel games and focus on ancestors (see Part 1 and Part 3), can make for a very fulfilling Power Hour. After implementing a Power Hour, you may conclude that one hour is not enough, decide to have a break, and gather again at another time of the day.

Simplify with Sunday Stations. Build into your Power Hour (or Power Half Hour) Sunday Stations where children rotate among four stopping places. The specific activities at the stations may be tailored to each family and can change from week to week. Sunday Stations entail rotating between 15-minute activities: for example, 15 minutes of "Sunday Service" (chapter 52); 15 minutes of "Exploring the Sources" (chapter 36); 15 minutes of "Gospel Art" (chapter 42); 15 minutes of "Jump to Journaling" (chapter 35).

Create a "Sabbath System." Having a Sabbath System can help you avoid re-inventing the wheel and ensure that you have a variety of high quality activities week after week to prevent children from becoming bored. In addition to providing a varied and simple routine, a Sabbath System ensures that certain important activities will be done at least once a month or once a quarter. While there are different ways you can do this, here's an example of how a Sabbath System might look:

> Each Sunday we plan to have a family council and study the scriptures together. We also want to do additional activities that will change based on the following structure: the first Sunday of the month, we will use an idea or two from "Special Guests and Field Trips"; on the second Sunday of the month, we will use an idea or two from "Gospel Games"; on the third Sunday, we will use an idea or two from "Family History Snowballing"; on the fourth Sunday, we will use one or two ideas from "Gospel Study."

Putting a system in place and even posting it on the wall allows everybody to know what you plan to do. Children get used to showing up at the appointed time, bringing scriptures, and enjoying this special time together. Take time to pick your favorite activities and plug them into your own Sabbath System. Your structure can work for a whole year (or longer!) and you can mix things up as you like. For additional information on "Sabbath Systems," refer to Appendix B.

Start Young, Start Now! Elder Bradley D. Foster taught: "It's never too early and it's never too late to lead, guide, and walk beside our children, because families are forever" ("It's Never Too Early and It's Never Too Late," *Ensign*, November 2015). Find encouragement in knowing that families with older children have successfully implemented more purposeful Sunday activities.

Some may wonder at what age they should start teaching their children. How young is too young? The answer is simple—no one is too young to begin learning the gospel. Elder David A. Bednar explained: "Youth of all ages, even infants, can and do respond to the distinctive spirit of the Book of Mormon. Children may not understand all of the words and stories, but they certainly can feel the 'familiar spirit' described by Isaiah (Isaiah 29:4; see also 2 Nephi 26:16)" ("Watching with All Perseverance," *Ensign*, May 2010).

Truthfully, the younger the children are, the easier it is to implement meaningful traditions. They grow up knowing that this is what their family does. Older children could resist such a change to what they expect on Sunday, but that does not mean all hope is lost! If your family is in this stage, I would suggest starting with one game from the Gospel Games section or with an activity from another section that has a fun feel. Begin with 10–15 minutes at a time and then gradually build from there. Gathering together when fun is involved can slowly help the habit and expectation form.

Certain Sabbath activities are only appropriate for one stage of life, and other activities span all ages. Try not to wish away any stage. You may be tired of "Scripture Land" (see chapter 2) or "Chutes and Ladders—Scripture Style" (see chapter 3), but sooner or later they will be tired of it too and then you may find yourself missing that simpler stage. You might be wishing for deeper doctrinal discussions with children, or longer attention spans. That time will also come. Enjoy each stage.

Along with this I add a caution. Beware of expecting too little. Generally, younger elementary-age children can search the scriptures, memorize, and remember details. If we are waiting on these types of activities until children seem more competent, we will be disappointed when we realize other challenges arise with older children. Too often when the increased capacity is apparent, the desire has decreased.

Sister Rosemary M. Wixom taught in general conference that we should teach our children five years before the time we want them to know those principles. She said, "What we want them to know five years from now needs to be part of our conversation with them today" ("Stay on the Path," *Ensign,* November 2010). For example, if you want them to know about proper dating when they are 16, then teach them at age 11. *For the Strength of Youth* (booklet, 2011) teachings really are very applicable to younger children.

A majority of the ideas presented in the following chapters span all ages. Some are geared to older children and some are more appropriate for younger children. Suggestions are provided to alter the activities for differently aged children. See Appendix A for a list of activities by age group.

Saturday Is Not Only a Special Day, It Is Vital. To have success on the Sabbath we need to remember that the Primary song is right—Saturday is a special day; it *is* a day to get ready for Sunday. The problem comes when we become too busy to really make this happen. We prepare extensively for events such as birthdays, special holidays, and other occasions that are important to us. We can be just as careful in weekly preparation for the sacred Sabbath. Simple rules like "No movies or 'hanging out' on Saturday night until the chores are done and things are ready for Sunday" better ensure that families are less distracted with unnecessary work on the holy Sabbath.

Having children set out Sunday clothes and shoes before going to bed on Saturday night can prevent frustration Sunday morning. Preparing meals earlier in the week, or choosing a simpler meal, can free up the hours spent cooking on Sunday. The individual things each of us will want to do may differ, but a key principle is to identify things that detract from your Sunday worship and find ways to take care of those things on a day other than the Sabbath. Additionally, taking the time to have personal spiritual renewal—perhaps with prayer and scripture study—can serve as the greatest catalyst for inviting the Holy Spirit.

Elder L. Tom Perry wisely taught: "Parents, now is the time to teach our children to be examples of the believers by attending sacrament meeting. When Sunday morning arrives, help them to be well rested, properly dressed, and spiritually prepared to partake of the emblems of the sacrament and receive the enlightening, edifying, ennobling power of the Holy Ghost" ("The Sabbath and the Sacrament," *Ensign*, May 2011).

For the Strength of Youth teaches: "Prepare during the week so that you can reserve Sunday for the many uplifting activities that are appropriate for the Sabbath day. Such activities include spending quiet time with your family, studying the gospel, fulfilling your Church callings and responsibilities, serving others, writing letters, writing in your journal, and doing family history work" (30).

Stay in Appropriate Sunday Dress. While appropriate dress does not need to be their most formal clothing, the day will feel different for your children when their attire differs from the other days of the week. Family members are more likely to act and behave in a manner that shows the Lord they treat His day differently. *For the Strength of Youth* counsels: "Your behavior and dress on the Sabbath should show respect for the Lord and His holy day" (30). Notice it does not say, "your behavior and dress *for church* should . . ." but instead uses the word *Sabbath*, referring to the day. For some families, this may mean staying in church clothes all day; for other families, it may mean changing into clothes that are still dressy but not their Sunday best. Dignified attire often leads to more dignified behavior.

Elder L. Tom Perry also taught: "I believe [the Lord] desires us to dress appropriately. Our youth may think the old saying 'Sunday best' is outdated. Still, we know that when Sunday dress deteriorates to everyday attire, attitudes and actions follow. Of course, it may not be necessary for our children to wear formal Sunday attire until the sun goes down. However, by the clothing we encourage them to wear and the activities we plan, we help them prepare for the sacrament and enjoy its blessings throughout the day" ("The Sabbath and the Sacrament," *Ensign*, May 2011).

Note: Following this section is a family home evening lesson outline that contains prophetic promises regarding the Sabbath. If your family is currently in the habit of gathering for meaningful time together and looks forward to the Sabbath, this sample lesson may not be necessary before implementing new ideas.

A Thought before We Begin

Of course, families can have a happy, sanctified Sabbath without ever playing any of the games in the Gospel Games section or celebrating any of the significant days presented. I hope you will never view the ideas presented in this book as mandatory or prescriptive, but rather use the ideas as a resource to assist you as you strive to keep the proper spirit of the Sabbath with children of varying needs and interests. If you would like to see video clips of ideas presented here and additional suggestions, please contact celebratesunday@gmail.com. I would love to hear from you.

I know when I have prayerfully and humbly sought to be more purposeful in the Sabbath—even with my meager ability—I have felt a power and peace directly connected with honoring the Lord's holy day.

Family Home Evening Lesson:
THE DOCTRINE OF THE HOLY SABBATH

NOTE: THIS LESSON CAN BE helpful to get all family members on the same page and solicit support for implementing new ideas. The discussion items below may be altered or omitted to meet your family's needs.

- Write the following images on a paper or whiteboard, and then ask family members what each of the signs means. X $ % * #

- Discuss the sign found in the scripture Ezekiel 20:20. What is the Sabbath a sign of? (Memorization tip: Just like if someone has 20/20 vision it means they have clear vision, Ezekiel 20:20 tells us how we see the Lord.)

- Ask what kind of sign we want to give Heavenly Father. Bear a simple testimony like: "I know the Lord has special blessings for us as we make a greater effort to show the Lord we love Him and honor Him on the Sabbath." Share the first and/or second quote and ask family members to listen for what activities are appropriate for Sunday.

- Develop your plan of action, or suggest a few of the activities you want to start with for your Power Hour (or Power Half-Hour). Ask family members if they are willing to jump on board.

- Ask them to listen for ideas as you read the third or fourth quote. (Notice, Isaiah commands us to turn away from "our pleasure.") After the quotes are read, have everyone think of one thing that could be considered their "own pleasure." Discuss what family members may need to give up so they have time and energy to devote to meaningful Sabbath activities.

1. "We make the Sabbath a delight when we teach the gospel to our children. Our responsibility as parents is abundantly clear. . . . As you teach the gospel, you will learn more. This is the Lord's way of helping you to comprehend His gospel. . . . Such study of the gospel makes the Sabbath a delight. This promise pertains regardless of family size, composition, or location" (Elder Russell M. Nelson, "The Sabbath Is a Delight," *Ensign* May 2015).

2. "We call upon parents to devote their *best efforts* to the teaching and rearing of their children in gospel principles which will keep them close to the Church. The home is the basis of a righteous life, and no other instrumentality can take its place or fulfill its essential functions in carrying forward this God-given responsibility. We counsel parents and children to give *highest priority* to family prayer, family home evening, *gospel study and instruction*, and wholesome family activities. However worthy and appropriate other demands or activities may be, they must not be permitted to displace the divinely-appointed duties that only parents and families can adequately perform" ("Letter from the First Presidency," February 11, 1999; emphasis added).

3. "When Isaiah described the Sabbath as 'a delight,' he also taught us how to make it delightful. He said: 'If thou turn away . . . from doing thy pleasure on my holy day; and call the sabbath a delight, . . . and shalt honour [the Lord], not doing thine own ways, nor finding thine own pleasure, nor speaking thine own words: Then shalt thou delight thyself *in the Lord*' (Isaiah 58: 13–14). Not pursuing your 'own pleasure' on the Sabbath requires self-discipline. You may have to deny yourself of something you might like. If you choose to delight yourself *in the Lord,* you will not permit yourself to treat it as any other day. Routine and recreational activities can be done some other time. . . . Faith in God engenders a love for the Sabbath; faith in the Sabbath engenders a love for God. A sacred Sabbath truly is a delight" (Elder Russell M. Nelson, "The Sabbath Is a Delight," *Ensign*, May 2015).

4. "We urge bishops and other Church officers to do all they can to assist parents in seeing that they have time and help, where needed, as they nurture their families and bring them up in the way of the Lord. Wherever possible, Sunday meetings, other than those under the three-hour schedule

and perhaps council meetings on early Sunday mornings or firesides later in the evening, *should be avoided* so that parents may be with their children. As we strengthen families, we will strengthen the entire Church ("Letter from the First Presidency," February 11, 1999; emphasis added).

Tip: You may consider using songs from Roger and Melanie Hoffman's music album *Sunday Day of Joy*, which teach principles of the Sabbath with kid-friendly tunes. Even without the songs, though, young children can understand the true principles presented above.

Part 1

GOSPEL GAMES

I tried to teach my child with books;
He gave me only puzzled looks.
I tried to teach my child with words;
They passed him by often unheard.
Despairingly I turned aside,
"How shall I teach this child?" I cried.
Into my hand he put the key.
"Come," he said, "Play with me."
Author Unknown

THE EXPRESSION "THE FAMILY THAT plays together stays together" can be particularly true on Sundays. I've found it is fun to modify the rules or characters of board games to give them a Sunday flair and differentiate them from how we might usually play them. There are countless ways you can do this. Use Legos to build temples or King Benjamin's tower; use puppets to show how to share or tell the truth; use dress ups for people in the scriptures, such as Captain Moroni or Queen Esther, to demonstrate faith and courage; modify a simple game of playing house where your small children teach their dolls Book of Mormon stories. These can all be fun Sabbath-appropriate activities for your children.

This section includes several games that families may enjoy playing together on Sunday. Some facilitate gospel learning and others simply have scriptural themes. Games toward the beginning of this section are well suited for children ages three and up. Games toward the end of the section are geared toward ages eight and up. Appendix A contains additional age-specific information.

The key for all of these gospel games (like all games!) is to end the game while it is still fun so players will be left wanting more—15 to 20 minutes is an effective time limit.

1

SCRIPTURE LAND

(ages 2–7)

Get Ready! Scripture Land is based on the game Candyland—a classic board game that never seems to get old for the young at heart. The pathway on the board winds through a variety of places with candy themes, such as Muddy Molasses Swamp, Frosty Fairyland, and Gumdrop Mountains. With Scripture Land, you can engage younger children in scripture language by playing this familiar game with scripture imagery instead.

Get Set! Materials needed: Candyland or a similar game board, scriptures, paper and pens, colored squares of paper or a spinner to move along the game board, and a game piece for each player.

Play! Instructions:

- Scripture Land is played the same as Candyland but with new labels for the "lands" and characters on the board. Children can brainstorm names of lands and people from the scriptures; for example: the Molasses Swamp might become the "Dreary Wilderness," the Peppermint Forest might become the "Tree of Life," Queen Frostine might be replaced by "Queen Esther," and Lord Licorice might become "Sneaky Satan."

- Write the new labels on pieces of paper and place them on the board.

- A player begins the game by drawing a card from the pile of colored cards and moving his game piece to the first square on the path that matches the color of the card drawn.

- Play continues clockwise until one player reaches the Candy Castle—which you may have renamed "Land Bountiful," "the Promised Land," or the temple.

Tip #1: With very young players, the parent or older sibling can create the new labels, and the younger child can choose where to place the labels along the colorful path.

Tip #2: For children 6 and older, play as above, but ask questions related to the lands each player passes. For example, as a player passes the "Tree of Life," ask, "What does the tree of life symbolize?" or "How can you feel the love of God?" If you chose the temple to replace the Candy Castle, ask, "Why do you want to be worthy to enter the temple?" When a player is near the "Dreary Wilderness" (the Molasses Swamp), ask, "How can you stay away from Satan's sticky traps?" These questions can change according to the types or names of places you choose and the age or knowledge of those playing.

2

REVERSE GOSPEL PICTIONARY

(ages 3 and up)

Get Ready! In this twist on Pictionary, everyone draws his or her own idea at the same time, and then all players take turns guessing what each person drew.

Get Set! Materials needed: Scratch paper and writing utensils (crayons or markers).

Play! Instructions:

- Give family members one or two minutes to draw a scripture scene, person, place, or object on their papers.

- The youngest player holds up his drawing first and the other players guess what it is.

- As soon as the correct answer is guessed, the illustrator shares a lesson that he has learned from the story or person he drew. For example, if he drew a picture of the Liahona, he might say, "Following the directions on the Liahona led Lehi's family to fertile parts in the wilderness, so we know that following God's directions will lead us to happier places." (Of course, the language of the "lesson" will be age appropriate.)

- The next youngest person in the circle reveals her drawing and the process is repeated until all players have displayed and explained their pictures.

Tip #1: You can encourage further sharing by asking for personal applications. For example, you might ask, "Tell about a time when following the Lord's directions brought you happiness."

Tip #2: Depending on the age of the children, it might be helpful to have gospel art pictures or scripture books to flip through for drawing ideas.

3

CHUTES AND LADDERS—SCRIPTURE STYLE

(ages 3 and up to play; ages 8 and up to prepare scriptures)

Get Ready! The original Chutes and Ladders game involves advancing player tokens along the board to reach the final destination, aided by ladders or impeded by slides along the way: reach the bottom of the ladder and you can move up to the top, skipping the spaces in between; stop your token at the top of the slide and you tumble to the bottom of the chute! To adapt this game for a gospel setting, use the scriptures to emphasize the rising and falling action inherent in the game-play. In preparation for the game, players should find their own scriptures that relate to the theme of going up or going down (details below). Older siblings and adults can assist younger children in searching for scriptures. The search for scriptures is part of what makes the game meaningful. Electronic devices are perfect for searching words and phrases.

Get Set! Materials needed: A Chutes and Ladders or similar game board, a game piece for each player, a list of scriptures that relate to rising or falling, spinner or die.

Play! Instructions:

- For older children, making the scripture-style game board is an important part of the activity. Players 8 and older may independently search for words or phrases using the electronic version of the scriptures or the Topical Guide. Search for words or phrases that have to do with "going up" a ladder or "falling down" a chute; for example, they might look up words or phrases like "lifted up," "rise," "build," "drag," "fall," and "thrust down." The players write scripture phrases and their references on strips of paper and place them in one of two groups: the falling group and the rising group.

- If your game board is large enough, place the scripture slips on the actual board in the appropriate places: the scriptures with phrases such as "it shall rise with you in the resurrection" are placed at the foot of a pictured ladder, and the scriptures such as "ye shall be thrust down to hell" are placed at the top of a pictured chute.

- With children younger than 7, the scriptures listed in Tip #2 may be used.

- The youngest person starts first. Using a spinner or die, the child moves her game piece along the board according to the number on the spinner/die. If the game piece lands on a square at the bottom of a ladder, the player's piece ascends to the top of the ladder, ending a few rows or squares closer to the finish. If the game piece lands on a square at the top of a slide (chute), the player's piece descends to the bottom of the slide, ending a few rows or squares closer to the start.

- An older player may read one of the appropriate scriptures when a player lands on a ladder or chute.

- While the game is under way, share simple statements of testimony confirming the truth of the scriptures used. One of the best things about searching for your own scriptures is that the game will be different every time you play it together.

Tip #1: Some versions of Chutes and Ladders game boards have illustrations spread throughout the board. For example, an image of a child helping someone fills the square at the bottom of an ascending ladder. On the squares at the beginning of a descending slide are images of children making unwise choices. Without using words, the game board itself teaches important principles. If the game board you have or decide to make does not have images on it, you can add your own. To help children internalize the principles from the scriptures, have them draw something from the scripture messages they find and place it in the appropriate place on the game board. They could draw an image that reminds them of the scripture they found or they could draw their own idea of a choice that would either make them rise or fall.

Depending on the interests of family members you may choose to play using only scriptures, or only illustrations, or a combination of both. However you choose to play, the underlying purpose is to get family members searching, thinking about, and internalizing the scripture passages they find.

Tip #2: Children younger than 7 can use these scriptures:

Ladder Scriptures: Psalms 121:1; Doctrine and Covenants 109:19; Isaiah 55:9; Doctrine and Covenants 75:16; 2 Corinthians 4:14.

Chute Scriptures: Alma 30:60; Matthew 7:27; 2 Nephi 9:34; Mormon 6:14.

4

SUNDAY CHARADES

(ages 4 and up)

Get Ready! Charades is a guessing game where clues are given through physical language rather than verbal language—acting without words. Sunday Charades is played using themes from the gospel and the scriptures. It may be played with an individual doing all the actions to represent a gospel story or character, or a group of 3 or 4 people may act as multiple characters in a scripture scene. Family members of all ages can happily participate, with each person being an active participant while either guessing or acting.

Get Set! Materials needed: for group charades—none!

Pictures or written labels of scripture characters are needed for the individual version (see instructions below).

Play!
Instructions for Group Sunday Charades:

If your family is large, split into two groups. Each group goes to a different room to decide on their charade and to plan how to act it out. Then the groups come back to the same room and perform for each other. If your family has fewer members, one person may guess while the others act.

After one group's charade is performed and guessed, the other group performs its charade; when the second charade is guessed, everyone separates for another round. You may want to take the opportunity to further discuss a story or person after the fun of performing is over. Sometimes this works well right after each performance, or it may conclude the activity after a few rounds are complete.

Instructions for Individual Sunday Charades:

Tape a picture (or written name, if everyone can read) of a scripture character on the back of each person. To help each person guess the name of the character that has been placed on his or her back, players take turns acting out characteristics or stories involving the characters.

Tip: This game works well when guests visit. The groups can get bigger and more creative. Samuel the Lamanite is a favorite one to act out, but children may need to be reminded that none of the rocks or arrows actually hit Samuel!

5

APPLES TO CHAPELS

(ages 6 and up)

Get Ready! The popular game Apples to Apples consists of one person, the judge, playing a card with an adjective (like "Silly") and other players finding a noun from their hand that fits the adjective (like "Animated Movies" or "Toy Cars"). The judge then chooses which noun he thinks best fits the adjective; then another person becomes the judge and the process is repeated. This game can be modified as a fun way to help children think creatively about different people, places, and things from the scriptures.

Get Set! Materials needed: A stack of noun cards (at least 30) and a stack of adjective cards (at least 100). If you own the game Apples to Apples, you may use the adjective cards it contains. Otherwise, make your own cards (an easy way to do this is to do an online search for "list of adjectives"). Using index cards of different colors works well for distinguishing between homemade "noun" and "adjective" cards (green cards for adjectives and red cards for nouns, for example).

On your noun cards, write the names of scriptural people or places. If you want to go the extra mile, have your children write a scripture reference on each noun card that corresponds to the scriptural person or place on the card.

Play! Instructions:

- Each player draws an agreed-upon number of adjective cards (usually 5 to 7) from a draw pile.

- As judge, the youngest person begins play by drawing one noun card and reading it out loud. (Children who cannot read may play on teams with other players.)

- The other players choose from their hands one of their adjective cards that they think best describes the selected noun. They hand their cards, word sides down, to the judge.

- The judge selects the adjective she thinks is most descriptive of the person or place and awards a point to the person whose adjective card was chosen. For example, after the judge reads the noun card that says, "King David," the other players each give her one of their adjective cards to describe "King David." The judge chooses the response she likes best.

- If a scripture reference is written on the card, this is the perfect time to read the verse about that scriptural character. If there are no written references, the person who won the round (i.e., whose adjective card was chosen) can share something the family can learn from that character.

- A new judge is appointed for the next round, each player draws another card from the adjective pile (to make a complete hand of 5 to 7 cards), and the next round begins.

Tip #1: Do not include members of the Godhead on your noun cards. This prevents disrespecting deity with inappropriate adjectives.

Tip #2: Part of the fun and learning comes from involving all players in making the cards—one hundred cards can be made in less than ten minutes. Some may have sloppy handwriting or will not be "Pinterest perfect" but that is okay—the purpose is to get everyone involved!

6

GOSPEL 20 QUESTIONS

(ages 6 and up)

Get Ready! The popular game 20 Questions is turned into scripture review and discussion.

Get Set! Materials needed: None.

Play! Instructions:

- One family member chooses a person, place, or thing found in the scriptures. She answers only "yes or no" questions from the other participants.

- Other players ask "yes or no" questions to find out the mystery word. The goal is to guess the correct answer before 20 questions are asked. One person may be designated to keep track of the number of questions asked.

- The person who guesses the correct answer chooses the person, place, or thing to be guessed in the next round.

- A game might go something like this:
    Question: Is it a person? Answer: No.
    Question: Is it bigger than a book? Answer: Yes.
    Question: Is it alive? Answer: No.
    Question: Is it in the Book of Mormon? Answer: Yes.
    Question: Is it in the first half of the Book of Mormon? Answer: Yes.
    Question: Is it in 1 Nephi? Answer: Yes.
    Question: Is it Laban's sword? Answer: No.
    Question: Is it the Liahona? Answer: No.
    Question: Is it Nephi's bow? Answer: No.
    Question: Is it bigger than a house? Answer: Yes.
    Question: Is it the boat Nephi built? Answer: YES!

Tip #1: If the players can tolerate a minute of seriousness between rounds, you may want to ask the group to consider a thoughtful question that follows up on the word selected, such as, "What can we learn from the story of Nephi building a boat?" A few answers may be given and a brief testimony shared: "I know the Lord can help us do things we have never done before." Then you are on to the next round.

Tip #2: Don't hesitate to include children of all ages. We have played with both preschoolers and older children in one big group and still have been successfully challenged by each other's answers and questions.

7

BIBLE BALDERDASH

(ages 6 and up)

Get Ready! Dive into lesser known Bible stories by making up definitions for people and places you are not familiar with. Then read the real definition and discuss the true meaning.

Get Set! Materials needed: Bible with Bible Dictionary, pieces of paper (index card size works well), and pens or pencils.

Play! Instructions:

- One person, the designated reader, chooses a word from the Bible Dictionary and reads it out loud. The reader tells the group whether the word is a person, place, or thing.

- Each player writes down a made-up definition of the word and passes the paper facedown to the reader.

- The reader writes the correct definition of the word on a piece of paper. He then compiles all the definitions together, both fabricated and correct definitions, and reads each of them out loud.

- Each player votes for the definition he thinks is correct. Then the reader identifies the correct definition. One point is awarded to a player for each person who votes for his false definition (thus players are motivated to make their definitions sound plausible). Two points are given to each person who votes for the correct definition and two points are earned by any player who writes down the correct definition but was not the reader. (Note: The reader may read through the definitions on his own prior to reading them aloud; if a player wrote the correct definition, the reader can discard his original.)

- After points are tallied, the reader tells the Bible story that goes along with the word, as found in the Bible Dictionary.

- The reader chooses a new word and round two begins.

Tip #1: You don't need a thorough knowledge of obscure Bible stories to play because the answers are often given clearly and succinctly in the Bible Dictionary. Preschoolers may participate by drawing pictures of what they think the given word is.

Tip #2: Depending on how competitive your kids are, you might consider playing without points.

8

SCRIPTURE BINGO

(ages 6 and up)

Get Ready! Children young and old love to play the classic game of Bingo. Scripture Bingo is played like regular Bingo, except that children create their own Bingo cards with scripture words or images they find.

Get Set! Materials needed: Bingo cards with 25 blank squares in five rows of five squares each (print a blank template from the Internet or make your own), beans or other markers to mark spaces, scriptures, paper, and writing utensils.

Play! Instructions:

- Ask family members to search the scriptures looking for objects they can easily draw, such as a trumpet (Doctrine and Covenants 24:12) or a lightbulb (Mosiah 16:9). Words for body parts such as *hands, feet, head, ear,* and *eye* are contained in countless scriptures and work well, as do words such as *rock, heart, bread, rain,* and *sun.*

- When the scriptures are found and related images chosen, the Bingo cards can be created. Everyone helps during this step. For a regular Bingo card, 25 squares are filled with one image in each square. If you have five players, each player will find five scriptural images and draw those five images on each of five cards. (If you have more or fewer people, adjust the number of images each player finds accordingly.)

- The players draw their number of images in different spaces on each of the Bingo cards.

- Each person may draw his or her images on a master sheet of paper that the caller will use to choose images from.

- When the master sheet includes 25 images, and images have been drawn on each Bingo card, the game begins with the caller calling out the first image. The players place a bean or other marker over that particular image on their cards.

- The caller continues to call out images, marking them off on the master sheet until someone calls out "BINGO!" A Bingo may be four corner squares covered or five squares in a row, up, down, or diagonally.

- During the course of the game, when a person's image is called, the person who selected that image may read the related verse aloud.

Tip #1: Your family may choose to use clipart from a computer program. Fill the squares as above, with one person appointed to find the clipart for the related objects. Print five copies of each image and paste them randomly on each of the five Bingo cards.

Tip #2: Words may be used instead of images, especially with older players.

9

SCRIPTURE SCRABBLE

(ages 7 and up)

Get Ready! Scripture Scrabble is played like regular Scrabble, but extra points are given for words from the scriptures. It is best played in paired teams. During Scripture Scrabble, if a team can find a word from the scriptures, then the word counts for double the points. For example, if the team wanted to use the word *hand*, according to Scrabble points the H is worth 2, A worth 1, N worth 3, and D worth 2. But because it is found in the scriptures (1 Nephi 1:3), instead of being worth 8 points it is worth 16. Additionally, if the word *hand* is laid down on the board over a square that reads, "double word score," then it is worth 32 points! While it is not mandatory to use a word from the scriptures, it is definitely advantageous.

Get Set! Materials needed: A regular Scrabble board or similar board and Scrabble letters.

Play! Instructions:

- Turn letters facedown. Each player takes 7 letters from the pile.
- Starting at the star in the center of the board, players take turns laying down letters to make words, connecting new words to words already on the board.
- After making a word, a player concludes her turn by replacing the number of letter tiles used, always having seven letters to work with.
- If a player cannot create a word, she may use that turn to exchange two letters with the draw pile.
- For variety, you can either allow any word found in the standard works, or if you would like your family to study a specific chapter, you can limit it to words found in that chapter.

- When a player chooses to use a word from the scriptures, they must read both the reference and the verse when laying down the word.

Tip #1: Electronic searches can make finding specific words easier. It is up to you if you want to encourage or limit use of electronics.

Tip #2: Additional points can be awarded for wods found in the doctrinal mastery verses.

10

WHERE IN THE WORLD IS DEBORAH?

(ages 8 and up)

Get Ready! Some years ago, "Where in the World Is Carmen Sandiego?" was a popular computer game designed to help elementary-school-age children learn geography facts. In a similar way, this game helps teach the geography of the Bible (or if you like, the Book of Mormon or modern Church history sites).

Get Set! Materials needed: Bibles with maps and paper and pens.

Play! Instructions:

- Show family members the maps of the biblical world (in the LDS edition of the Bible or find your own). Decide which map you will use so that everyone is studying the same map.

- Each person writes five questions about five different cities or places on the map. Each question should include a scripture reference "clue" where the answer may be found (locate clues by looking up locations in the Bible Dictionary, using the electronic version of the scriptures, or the explanation page adjacent to the map in the LDS Bible). Sample questions might be the following:
    1. "Where did Jesus heal a lame man on the Sabbath? (For a clue, go to John 5:2–9.)"
    2. "What is the name of Paul's hometown? He went here for protection. (For a clue, go to Acts 9:29–30.)"
    3. "What is the name of this island where Paul was unharmed by a snakebite? (For a clue, read Acts 28: 1–9.)"

- Players take turns asking the questions. Since the purpose of this game is to facilitate learning, it is an open book game—family members may refer to the map and explanations to find the answers to the questions.

- For older players, keep track of points. If a player answers a question correctly without scripture references or clues, five points are awarded. If the player receives additional information or clues before answering correctly, three points are awarded. Fifteen points wins the game.

Tip #1: Cities do not need to be read or "traveled to" in any particular order. Tailor the game to fit the needs of your family. Let family members modify the rules to suit their abilities and interests. Feel free to save the clues each time you play and soon you will have a collection for a larger scale game to play as a review for your family.

Tip #2: You can change the name of the game, depending on which maps you use. For example, in the LDS edition of the Bible, Maps 3 and 4 could be titled "Where in the World Is King David?" while Map 10 could be called "Where in the World Is Deborah?" Maps 11 through 13 could be used for "Where in the World Is the Apostle Paul?" Church history maps (found in the back of the LDS triple edition) could be used for "Where in the World Is Lucy Mack Smith?"

11

THE MAGIC SUNDAY SQUARE

(ages 8 and up)

Get Ready! This fun game may be used to help your children learn key verses of scripture or scriptures about any gospel topic you want to emphasize. It keeps children's attention while important topics are reviewed. While it may seem complicated at first, try it out and enjoy the simplicity. The characters themselves are not a key part of the game play—you just need four good guys and a bad guy, so feel free to choose your own characters. Using the appropriate initials, assign the points you want to each character, along with the corresponding number of boxes dedicated to each one. It might be more fun for children if they choose their own characters, too, because the character selection could reinforce their family or personal scripture study.

Get Set! Materials needed: a copy of the blank Magic Sunday Square for each player (created from the example below), a blank sheet of paper for each player, writing utensils, and a list of 25 questions covering a gospel topic. These could be questions about a book of scripture, a gospel topic, a doctrinal mastery verse, an ancestor, etc.

Play! Instructions:

- Each player receives a blank Magic Sunday Square and fills in four "good" scriptural characters (like Miriam, Ruth, Esther, and King Solomon) and one "bad" character (like Cain). All players must use the same five characters. They assign each character a certain number of points (100, 50, 25, 10, and Lose All Points), then randomly fill in all the empty squares of their grid using the first initial of the characters' names (in this case, the letters M, R, E, S and C) in the quantities indicated below.

- One person, the moderator, places small pieces of paper with the 25 individual coordinates in a bowl: A1, A2, A3, A4, A5, B1, B2, etc.

- The moderator asks a question from the list.

- Players have a set amount of time (20 seconds, for example) to write down the answer to the question on their separate piece of paper.

- The moderator announces the correct answer, identifies which players had the correct answer, and then picks a random paper with a coordinate from the bowl (A1, A2, B1, B2, etc.).

- Players who answered the question correctly receive the number of points related to the character in their box that had the coordinates the moderator just chose, and they write the point total on their sheet. For example, if the box coordinates chosen from the bowl were C1, and S was in C1 on their grid (see sample grid), they would receive 10 points. But beware: If a square with C for Cain is chosen and the player got the answer correct, all points are lost. (Players do not know if it is advantageous to answer correctly until the moderator chooses the grid coordinates.)

- Those who did not answer the question correctly do not gain or lose any points, and they leave that square and its points unused.

- The moderator asks another question and the process is repeated. Players keep a running total of their points on their sheets next to their grids.

- The player with the most points at the end wins. Competition is at a minimum because of the possibility of losing all your points even if you answer the questions correctly.

MAGIC SUNDAY SQUARE (Blank)

	A	B	C	D	E
1					
2					
3					
4					
5					

Five letters to be filled in randomly on the grid in the amount below:

1 of Miriam "M"	= 100 Points
5 of Ruth "R"	= 50 Points each
5 of Esther "E"	= 25 Points each
10 of King Solomon "S"	= 10 Points each
4 of Cain "C"	= Lose All Points

FILLED MAGIC SUNDAY SQUARE.

This is only a sample and should not be copied. Each player's grid will have the letters filled in a different order, whatever order they chose, but to be fair each player must have the correct amount of initials listed above. Only one "M" worth 100 points, and only 5 "R"s etc.

	A	B	C	D	E
1	S	R	S	S	S
2	S	M	C	S	R
3	R	E	S	R	S
4	E	C	S	S	C
5	C	E	E	R	E

Note: The points assigned to different scripture characters is just for fun and does not mean that Ruth is better than Esther or not as good as Miriam. Feel free to change the scripture characters, but keep the quantities and points as indicated.

Tip #1: One easy way to generate questions is to use the doctrinal mastery verses. For reference, each player may be given a printout of the book-marks found at http://seminary.lds.org containing the doctrinal mastery verses (25 for each of the standard works). Another way to generate questions is come up with review questions from your recent family scripture study. Have each family member contribute a few questions beforehand or one person look through the previous sections read and come up with the questions as the game is played.

Tip #2: You may use this to teach facts about ancestors (see chapter 31 on "Ancestor Anniversaries and Birthdays"). If a grandparent is visiting, they may ask questions based on their life and the questions are created in the moment or from a family history question list (see chapter 34 on "Family History Live Recordings").

Tip #3: To see a video example of this game email celebratesunday@ gmail.com

12

SCRIPTURE SPORTS

Scripture Basketball
(ages 8 and up)

Get Ready! Practice finding scriptures (or books of scripture) and shoot baskets before the time runs out.

Get Set! Materials needed: "Balls" of scrunched up paper or folded socks, a clean trash can or basket, and scriptures for each player.

Play! Instructions:

- Divide your family into two teams if your family size permits, or play the game with two players.

- Family members practice finding key verses of scripture or books of scripture. Each player may be given a printout of the doctrinal mastery bookmarks found at http://seminary.lds.org. These bookmarks will provide references for 25 key scripture verses, or they may be used to help family members become familiar with the books of the Bible.

- One person, the moderator, states aloud either a book from the Bible or a doctrinal mastery key word. One team searches their scriptures to find the specific reference or book of scripture. Team members may help each other.

- While one team is searching, players on the other team shoot baskets with the wadded-up paper or socks into the trash can. They keep shooting and scoring points until everyone on the first team finds the key word or book.

- The next round begins and the roles are reversed. The second team searches for scriptures while the first team shoots baskets. Players are motivated to search quickly so the other team has less time to score baskets.

- You may write down the scores for each round or choose to ignore the points and play noncompetitively.

Scripture Golf
(ages 8 and up)

Get Ready! As in the game of golf, the goal is to get the lowest score possible while finding key scripture passages or books in the Bible or Book of Mormon. Like Scripture Basketball, this game will familiarize your children with the location of books within the scriptures (for example, "Where is the book of Jeremiah?") or specific verses. The important point is to forget about the golf clubs, break out Scripture Golf this Sunday, and watch your children flip through the scriptures with amazing speed!

Get Set! Materials needed: A timer (if desired) and a set of scriptures for each player.

Play! Instructions:
- Each player is given a copy of the scriptures and, if using seminary scripture bookmarks, a bookmark with the doctrinal mastery references (found at http://seminary.lds.org).

- Announce a book of scripture or a doctrinal mastery verse to be looked up, and start the timer.

- The number the timer reaches when a player has found the correct place is his or her score (the lower the score, the better; lowest score wins).

Tip #1: The game may be tailored to span all age groups by creating a handicap for older children. For example, if an older player is required to add his age to his score for a particular round this may create a more level playing field.

Tip #2: Avoid competition by not keeping score.

13

CONFERENCE JEOPARDY!

(ages 8 and up)

Get Ready! Involve the entire family by letting each family member create questions based on conference talks. Older siblings and parents may assist younger ones.

Get Set! Materials needed: Printed or electronic versions of conference talks, paper, pencils, and a grid such as the one below.

Play! Instructions:

- Players write five questions based on talks from the most recent conference. Questions are worth 100, 200, 300, 400, and 500 points. The questions worth 500 points are the most challenging; questions worth 100 points are the least challenging.

- Modify the television *Jeopardy!* game by placing each family member's name at the head of a column, with the points 100 to 500 in the rows under each name (see the table below). Or place all the children's names across the top, with Mom and Dad acting as moderators (or alter the game in a way that fits your family).

- Split the family into two teams, or family members may compete as individuals.

- Begin from youngest to oldest. Players call for a question to answer from any column except their own. For example, "Mom, may I have your 200-point question?" Mom reads her 200-point question to the players.

- The player who first answers the question correctly receives the question's number of points and chooses the next question.

Dad	Mom	Child #1	Child #2	Child #3
100	100	100	100	100
200	200	200	200	200
300	300	300	300	300
400	400	400	400	400
500	500	500	500	500

Tip: This game may be easiest to play on the Sunday following conference, while the messages are still fresh in everybody's mind.

Part 2

SIGNIFICANT DATES/ANNIVERSARY CELEBRATIONS

"I HOPE THAT . . . WE ALWAYS celebrate with a purpose. I pray that we will make our celebrations more meaningful by reaffirming significant spiritual, political, cultural and social values" (Elder L. Tom Perry, *Living with Enthusiasm*, [Salt Lake City: Deseret Book, 1996], 82).

Children of all ages love celebrating! When I first had preschoolers at home I was amazed at how excited they were to see the decorations for a new holiday displayed, and their eager anticipation for celebrations no matter how simple they were. I realized that there were many spiritual celebrations we could implement that would help my children learn and get excited about the gospel.

One reason that Jews celebrate Passover is to teach children about an important event in their history, while reminding them of God's power and love for His children. Most traditions that go along with the Passover have meaning and purpose but some are just for fun, so the children can look forward to the day and find delight. Just as this is helpful for Passover, there are special days we can use to reaffirm "significant spiritual, political, cultural, and social values" like Elder Perry hoped.

While some of these significant dates might fall on a weekday, celebrating and remembering them on the Sunday nearest the date adds a little spice to our Sabbath activities. We also have the option of doing more involved activities on the actual day if it falls during the week. The great thing about this is no one will complain about more celebrating!

14

LOVE LEGACY—FEBRUARY

Main Idea: Days around Valentine's Day (February 14th) are filled with excitement! The children are busy writing the names of every class member on cards and anticipating all the candy they will receive. Capitalize on this excitement by increasing family love and teaching of God's love! A focus on the love of God in all its simplicity can turn this month of love into a meaningful time of year.

The Details: Consider some of the following activities for any Sunday in February.

- Memorize scriptures or scripture phrases like, "If ye love me, keep my commandments" (John 14:15) and "Thou shalt love the Lord thy God with all thy heart, and with all thy soul, and with all thy mind. . . . And the second is like unto it, Thou shalt love thy neighbour as thyself" (Matthew 22:37, 39). Every person would be blessed to have these scriptures in their heart and know them well.

- Have secret service pals (See chapter 52 "Sunday Service").

- Invite each person in the family to write his or her name on separate large hearts. Then every child can write what they love about the person whose name is on the particular heart. Hang the hearts in the house from the ceiling for at least a week and enjoy the feeling that comes from being surrounded by kind, uplifting words.

- Spread the joy outside your own family. Have everyone cut out simple paper hearts and put the names of neighbors or close friends on them. Go through the same process as described above, with each person writing one thing on the heart that they love about the chosen neighbors.

Try to secretly hang them in their house if you know them well or outside of their house if it is more appropriate.

- Heart attack your own walls (or your neighbor's front door) with hearts that have scripture verses about love written on them. For example, John 3:16, John 14:15, and 1 Peter 1:22 are a few of the hundreds of options that contain short, powerful love phrases. The Topical Guide is a great resource for this.

- Possible songs to sing while cutting, writing, and hanging hearts: "Love One Another" (*Hymns,* no. 308); "Love at Home" (*Hymns,* no. 294); "God Is Love" (*Hymns,* no. 87); "O Love That Glorifies the Son" (*Hymns,* no. 295); "Our Savior's Love" (*Hymns,* no. 113); "God Loved Us, So He Sent His Son" (*Hymns,* no. 187); Primary songs like "God's Love," "Love is Spoken Here," "I Feel My Savior's Love," and "Where Love Is."

Tip #1: These activities can clearly dominate multiple Sundays in February since we can never focus too much on scriptures teaching about God's love and loving others.

Tip #2: You may decide to use the same hearts more than one year in a row—not only to be frugal but also to remember what people wrote the previous year! Store them with your other February decorations.

15

THE PUBLICATION OF THE
BOOK OF MORMON—MARCH 26, 1830

Main Idea: The miraculous publication of The Book of Mormon deserves a few minutes of joyful remembrance and heartfelt testimony.

The Details: There are many ways to implement celebrations this day. Consider some of the following activities:

- Create something like reformed Egyptian characters with watercolor paint, crayons, playdough, etc. Search online to find and print samples of Egyptian characters to use as models. Older children can fold a piece of tin foil in half and double it over a piece of cardboard, then use a toothpick to "engrave" characters. They may even write a verse of scripture in their own language—a great idea for the small children. While your children are occupied painting and writing, talk to them about what a miracle it was that Joseph Smith could translate the Book of Mormon.

- Have a family member dress up as a character in the Book of Mormon and read a verse of scripture spoken by that character. Other family members guess which character they are.

- Play Book of Mormon story charades. Silently act out stories from the Book of Mormon either individually or in groups. Different family members may guess what story is being enacted.

- Use Monopoly money to show the children how much money it cost to publish the book back then ($3,000) and how much money it would be today (almost $73,000, see http://www.in2013dollars. com/1830-dollars-in-2013?amount=3000). Talk about the faith and testimony Martin Harris must have had to be willing to mortgage his farm and pay such a large amount.

- Act out the account of the three witnesses and eight witnesses found in the front pages of the Book of Mormon. Remind children to be respectful when acting out a visit from a heavenly messenger. Discuss how significant it is that none of them denied their testimony of the book even though many left the Church, which would have made it easy to deny the event, if it hadn't happened. (Consider also relating which witnesses later returned to the Church.)

- Ask each person to share a favorite Book of Mormon story, why it is their favorite, and/or something they learn from the story.

- Make treats shaped like the Book of Mormon, like a cake with reformed Egyptian characters written as part of the decoration, or the title written in gold on blue frosting.

Tip: There are many ways to implement celebrations this day, but the key is to take the opportunity to teach and testify of the truthfulness of The Book of Mormon. Even if you are only able to acknowledge the significance of the day and bear a brief testimony, the day will be a success.

16

THE RETURN OF ELIJAH—APRIL 3, 1836

Main Idea: Elijah is one of only a few people who are mentioned in *every* standard work. More than two thousand years ago it was prophesied that Elijah would return to the earth—and he has! At a sacred Sabbath meeting in the newly dedicated Kirtland Temple, Elijah appeared and gave Joseph Smith the sealing keys (see D&C 110). These sealing keys have changed the world.

The Details: The more fun your celebration is, the more likely it is that everyone will anticipate and remember it. Possible activities could include some of the following:

- Act out the story of when Elijah multiplied the widow's oil and raised the boy from the dead (1 Kings 17).

- Respectfully act out the account of the priests of Baal and when Elijah called fire down from heaven. Make it apparent that it was one person—Elijah—against 450 priests of Baal! Toy army men or Legos could illustrate the unequal numbers. Or have everyone in the family on one side of the room and one person representing Elijah on the other (see 1 Kings 18:22–40).

- Use a fan as a visual aid to represent the wind in the account from 1 Kings 19:11–12. If you turn the fan to the most turbulent speed and blow it on a family member's hair, the effect of the fan is obvious. Then turn the knob to the weakest level and direct the fan to a family member's hair (long hair is best) just for two seconds. Ask them if they can still see the effect of the fan. Testify how this is like the still small voice mentioned in 1 Kings 19. Sometimes we desire the huge burst of wind but a small breeze is just as real even if it may be harder to discern.

- For older children, have them look up Malachi 4:5–6 on http://scriptures.byu.edu. This website will point your children to general conference talks that have used these verses about the return of Elijah. Allow children to share with the family what they have learned.

- Have family members hold two strong magnets together and see if they can break them apart. Ask them how this is like or unlike the sealing power. For example, sealing powers can draw us closer together, just as magnets can be drawn together (magnets are like sealing). If you try to put the resistant sides of the magnets together, they will not stick together (magnets are not like sealing).

Personal note: One April morning I was flipping through the Doctrine and Covenants and asked out loud, "I wonder what day it was when Elijah actually returned." My five-year-old daughter looked up at me with the sincerest curiosity and exclaimed, "Who is Elijah?" In the process of commemorating a significant date I was able to teach my daughter the importance of Elijah and his faith-promoting stories. Additionally, my own faith was rekindled.

17

THE BIRTHDAY OF THE CHURCH—APRIL 6, 1830

Main Idea: April 6th is an important and sacred day. With a few simple traditions, it can be an edifying and memorable day. The Church was organized on April 6, 1830 (see Doctrine and Covenants 20). Because of the significance of the events on April 6, prophets and Apostles have scheduled other events for this day as well. For example, on 6 April, 1853, the cornerstone of the Salt Lake Temple was dedicated. Exactly 40 years later, on 6 April, 1893, President Wilford Woodruff dedicated the completed temple.

The Details: Choose one or more of the following activities to bring fun and significance to this day:

- Have a birthday celebration complete with cupcakes, candles, and singing "Happy Birthday" to the Church.

- Go to section 21 of the Doctrine and Covenants, which was the revelation given that day to the entire church. After reading verses 4–6, discuss how the first and only commandment given to the Church on this historic day was to follow the prophet.

- Testify that the three promises given in D&C 21:6 are really true: the gates of hell will not prevail against us, the Lord will disperse the power of darkness from before us, and He will cause the heavens to shake for our good. Depending on the attention span at the moment, share specific ways those promises have been true for your family as you have followed the prophet.

- Re-enact or read the following account:
    At the appointed hour, close to sixty people assembled to witness the formal organization of the Church of Jesus Christ. Approximately twenty of these people had come

from Colesville, a distance of approximately one hundred miles, to participate in the events of this sacred occasion. . . . After kneeling in solemn prayer, Joseph asked those present if they were willing to accept him and Oliver as their teachers and spiritual advisers. Everyone raised their hands in the affirmative. . . . Several individuals were baptized on that eventful day, including Orrin Porter Rockwell, Martin Harris, and Joseph Smith's parents. It was a time of joy and happiness in the life of the Prophet, who exclaimed, "Praise to my God! that I lived to see my own father baptized into the true Church of Jesus Christ!" (*Church History in the Fulness of Times* [Church Educational System Manual, 2003], 68)

Whatever you decide to do, be sure to testify of the Restoration and share your gratitude for the restored gospel. It will assuredly be a very happy occasion!

18

SUNDAYS PRECEDING EASTER, PALM SUNDAY, AND EASTER SUNDAY—MARCH/APRIL

Main Idea: Celebrate the holiest days in Christendom with unique and meaningful activities. John the Beloved dedicated more than a third of his entire gospel to the last week of the Savior's life. We can likewise dedicate a significant part of our energy to celebrate this sacred time.

The Details: *A week before Palm Sunday*—consider the following activities.

- Announce that the holiest time of year is near.

- Give a brief overview of the upcoming holy days so everyone can start anticipating.

- Put up pictures of the life of Christ, especially from the last week of His life. Give an introduction of these pictures and events in preparation for the weeks ahead.

- Print coloring pages of the Savior's life for young children from friend. lds.org. These can serve as some of the décor for the season.

- Just as Christmas music enhances our celebration of Christmas, music can also perform the same important function at Eastertime. Consider the *Stories of Jesus* music album by Roger and Melanie Hoffman with especially catchy songs for children, Robert Gardner's oratorio "Lamb of God," and the Mormon Tabernacle Choir Easter songs available for free online.

Palm Sunday—Palm Sunday occurs a week before Easter and commemorates when Jesus returned to Jerusalem for the last time in mortality.

- Act out the triumphal entry with paper cutouts (or real) palm branches, clothes "strewn in the way," and perhaps even a lot of joyful shouting! (See John 12)

- Review the events of Holy Week with gospel art pictures and scriptures. If you did this activity on the week prior, you may want to use the Sunday as a review and see which family members can teach/remember the events of the week: Monday—Jesus cleansed the temple (Matthew 21:12–13); Tuesday—He taught parables (Matthew 21:28–44); Thursday—Jesus presided at the Last Supper (Luke 22:8–20), and suffered in the Garden of Gethsemane (Luke 22:39–44); Friday—Jesus was crucified (Luke 23:32–46); Saturday—Jesus visited spirits in the spirit world while His body was in the tomb (1 Peter 3:18–20); Sunday morning—He was resurrected (Luke 24:1–10)!

Easter Sunday—The most glorious Sunday of the year! A morning sunrise devotional with Resurrection Rolls[1] while reading the New Testament accounts of Christ's first visitation as the resurrected Lord can be a great start to the day. The Hoffmans' upbeat and jubilant "He is Risen!" song is perfect for waking sleepy heads on this historic joyful morning.

- Include fish and honeycomb (or honey) as part of Easter Dinner to recreate what Jesus actually ate that evening with His Apostles when He appeared to them (see Luke 24:41–43).

- Act out the Resurrection morning scenarios in a way similar to how you might act out the nativity on Christmas. There are four versions: Matthew 28, Mark 16, Luke 24, and John 20. Costumes and hymns may be included.

Tip #1: Decide which fun and more serious activities you want to do on Palm Sunday and Easter Sunday; schedule them in to avoid being caught by surprise. While you are scheduling, refer to the following chapter on the seven Sundays following Easter.

Tip #2: Read *A Christ-Centered Easter* by Joe and Janet Hales for numerous additional ideas on how to focus on the Savior during the Easter season. *The Holy Week for Latter-day Saint Families* by Wendee Wilcox Rosborough is an additional resource.

---

1   These are so called because they are hollow in the center like the empty tomb. Do a quick internet search for the recipe; it simply entails placing a large marshmallow in the center of any type of bread dough and then baking the roll as usual.

19

THE SEVEN SUNDAYS FOLLOWING EASTER—APRIL/MAY

Main Idea: Do you ever cry the day you take the Christmas tree down? I do! I have often felt the same sadness when Easter Sunday draws to a close. That was the case until I realized that the days and weeks following Easter also have special significance. The Savior did not just appear on Easter Sunday but many times thereafter, especially during the ensuing weeks!

The Details:

A week after Easter—Additional appearances by the Savior. Eight days after Easter Sunday, the Savior appeared to His disciples the second time. In this instance, Thomas was there!

- Invite your family to pretend they are in the room when Jesus appears again. Ask them to make the facial expression they would have made. Have everyone share how they would feel if they were Thomas. Have them share how they would feel if they were one of the other disciples who had seen him the previous Sunday.

- Read John 20:26–31 and discuss how we can believe in the Savior even though we have not seen Him in this life.

- Color or draw pictures of Jesus appearing to his disciples again.

- Consider eating celebratory food from Jesus' time: fish, nuts, cheese, grapes, hummus, grape juice (white grape juice is more kid-friendly).

The second Sunday after Easter—Feed my sheep. You may discuss the account in John 21:1 which states: "After these things Jesus shewed himself again to the disciples at the sea of Tiberias." This is the setting in which Jesus gave His disciples the command to "feed my lambs" and "feed my sheep." The sermon in John 21 deserves at least annual reflection.

- For young children, you may choose to incorporate the sheep theme with a craft or treat to add creative fun. Cotton balls, cauliflower, or simple coloring pages may be in order.

- Discuss these questions: Who are the sheep? Who are the lambs? Where do we get the food to feed them? How do we feed them?

- Read and discuss Elder Jeffrey R. Holland's insights from his talk featuring this event (see "The First Great Commandment," *Ensign*, November 2012).

- Set a goal of something you can do this Sabbath day to show the Lord you love Him and you will feed His sheep. Then go and do it!

The third Sunday after Easter—Go ye into all the world. Only a few of the Savior's post-Resurrection commandments are recorded. One of these was, "Go ye into all the world, and preach the gospel to every creature" (Mark 16:15).

- Display a map of the world or print world maps as coloring pages for young children as you discuss this teaching of Jesus. If your map is laminated, you may choose to write names of relatives over the country in which they served missions, or you can simply point out places where family members, ancestors, or ward members have served.

- Reflect on the joy missionary work has brought you and your family. Share recent missionary experiences you have had as a family or as individuals.

- Discuss how your family can better fulfill this commandment.

The fourth and fifth Sundays after Easter—Hundreds of witnesses. The Apostle Paul tells us that the resurrected Christ appeared to many others besides His Apostles and close friends and associates in Jerusalem. Consider some of the following activities:

- Read 1 Corinthians 15:4–8, which describes several eyewitnesses of the resurrected Christ that we don't often discuss. Talk about what it means to be a witness and why the Savior would choose to show Himself to certain people. Why did He need witnesses then? Why does He need witnesses today? How can each of us be a witness of the Savior?

- Role-play a court scene with a judge and a witness for a made-up trivial case (like "Who took the cookies from the cookie jar?"). Let people take turns being the witness and questioning the witness. Discuss what a witness is.

- Remind family members that when we partake of the sacrament, we promise to be witnesses of the Savior. If feasible, visit the sacrament preparation room or the sacrament table in the chapel. Invite those who so desire to bear witness of the Savior (or, in other words, bear testimony). Sing "Testimony" (*Hymns*, no. 137), looking for phrases that stand out. The different setting may not be necessary but can serve as a catalyst for increased thoughtfulness in discussing this ordinance.

- Allow for personal journaling so family members can record how they can be a better witness of the Savior now, and/or what they can do to witness of Him in the future.

The sixth Sunday after Easter—The Ascension. Even though Acts 1:3 states that the Savior was seen of his Apostles "for forty days," because of the symbolic meaning of forty days it may not mean that exact time period. Nevertheless, Christian calendars mark the Day of Ascension 39 days after Easter, making it fall on a Thursday. Most celebrations happen on the Sunday following this Thursday; this ends up being six Sundays after Easter.

- Read the account in Acts 1:1–11. Act out the angels testifying to the Savior's disciples that Jesus will come again.

- Make lists of the signs of the Second Coming by searching in the Topical Guide for "Signs of the Second Coming."

- Sing the Primary song, "I Wonder When He Comes Again"; draw or paint pictures of what the Second Coming might be like.

- Invite family members to record in their personal journals how they imagine they will feel when the Savior returns or what they want to change in their lives before that time arrives.

The seventh Sunday after Easter—The Day of Pentecost. Celebrated seven Sundays after Easter Sunday, Pentecost commemorates the account in Acts 2. This is the day when the Apostles were filled with the Holy Ghost and the gift of tongues was manifest.

- Read the account in Acts 2; talk about the miracles that occurred. Discuss how the Holy Ghost can be felt in powerful ways and also in quiet ways (see chapter 16 on "The Return of Elijah" for a suggestion on illustrating this).

- Sing the Primary song "The Holy Ghost" or "Let the Holy Spirit Guide" (*Hymns,* no. 143), both of which list specific roles of the Holy Ghost. Discuss what the Holy Ghost does in our lives: comforts, testifies, teaches, warns, inspires, instructs, provides peace and assurance. Have all who desire share a variety of experiences of feeling the Holy Ghost.

- Read till the end of Acts 2, highlighting verses 14–18, with Peter's bold testimony, and verse 41, which declares that 3,000 were baptized that day. Wow!

20

THE RESTORATION OF THE PRIESTHOOD—MAY 15, 1829

Main Idea: May 15, 1829, was a historic and unusually wonderful day—definitely one important enough to acknowledge and commemorate with your family! John the Baptist conferred the Aaronic Priesthood on Joseph Smith and Oliver Cowdery. A short time later, the Melchizedek Priesthood was restored by Peter, James and John (see Doctrine and Covenants 27:12–13). Additionally, priesthood keys were restored on April 3, 1836, as part of other angelic appearances (see D&C 110). The priesthood—the authority to act in God's name—needed to be restored before the Church could be organized about a year later.

Oliver Cowdery, witness to the Book of Mormon, wrote the following:

> I was present with Joseph when an holy angel from God came down from heaven and conferred on us, or restored, the lesser or Aaronic Priesthood, and said to us, at the same time, that it should remain upon the earth while the earth stands. I was also present with Joseph when the higher or Melchizedek Priesthood was conferred by the holy angel from on high. This Priesthood, we then conferred on each other by the will and commandment of God" (*History of the Church* 1:41, footnote, as quoted on history.lds.org).

The Details: Possible activities to commemorate this event could include one or a few of the following:

- Take a field trip to a nearby river to reflect and discuss the events that took place on the banks of the Susquehanna River.

- Challenge your kids to memorize an entire section from the Doctrine and Covenants. Before they start begging for mercy, have them turn to Section 13, which is just one verse. Memorize it! (See chapter 41 for memorization tips.)

- Talk for a few minutes about the children's baby blessings, baptisms, and other priesthood blessings family members or ancestors have received. Discuss how the priesthood has blessed your family.

- Give the reminder that one component of the priesthood is serving others, and discuss as a family who you can serve. Then go serve them today (see chapter 52 "Sunday Service" for ideas).

- Watch the five-minute Mormon Messages video clip entitled "The Restoration of the Priesthood," which gives a succinct review of the sacred events (see http://www.youtube.com/watch?v=Wkp4WstIBCI).

- For creative fun, think of treats that start with the letter P: popcorn, peanuts, pies, pretzels, pink lemonade, pecans, and peaches. Choose one or two to enjoy together while you discuss the priesthood.

21

THE ORGANIZATION OF THE PRIMARY—AUGUST 25, 1878

Main Idea: Remind family members of the many blessings we enjoy today because of the Primary organization.

Aurelia Spencer Rogers, a 44-year-old mother of 12, felt strongly that something should be done about the behavior of the neighborhood boys who ran freely through the town day and night. She felt many of these children were not being taught basic principles and values and therefore would not be prepared in either knowledge or behavior to carry the gospel forward, or even to be good parents or citizens.

Sister Rogers discussed her concerns and a plan of action with general Relief Society president Eliza R. Snow. With the approval of President John Taylor and after receiving a calling from her bishop, Sister Rogers began planning for the first meeting of the Primary Association. Since these leaders decided that "singing was necessary," girls were also invited to "make it sound as well as it should." ("History of Primary," https://www.lds.org/callings/primary/getting-started/history-of-primary?lang=eng)

The Details: Commemorative ideas for this important date may include the following:

- Memorize some of "My Gospel Standards" (*Friend*, August 2009) in sections. Take five minutes at breakfast, lunch, and dinner and see how many standards you can remember at each meal. You may reward those who participate.

- Visit the LDS Primary website. Review the topics of this year's Sharing Time themes.

- Have parents or grandparents tell their memories of Primary, favorite Primary teachers, or favorite Primary songs.

- Sing everyone's favorite Primary songs.

- Invite children to share what one of their most memorable Primary lessons has been.

- Prepare a short devotional revolving around the simple truths taught in Primary.

- Discuss the benefits of Activity Days and Cub Scouts. Parents may share a memory of these activities in their younger years.

- Take the time today to invite a child who hasn't ever been to Primary, or who hasn't been to Primary in a while, to come to Primary!

22

THE APPEARANCE OF ANGEL MORONI AND JOSEPH
OBTAINING THE GOLDEN PLATES—SEPTEMBER 21–22

Main Idea: Remember and commemorate these significant events that occurred by sharing simple testimony and engaging in appropriate activities.

Joseph Smith testified, "On the evening of the . . . twenty-first of September [1823], . . . I betook myself to prayer and supplication to Almighty God. . . . While I was thus in the act of calling upon God, I discovered a light appearing in my room, which continued to increase until the room was lighter than at noonday" (Joseph Smith History 1:29–30).

In the next three pages of his testimony, Joseph Smith recounts the details surrounding additional visits of the Angel Moroni over the next 12 hours. When Joseph went to obtain the plates, Moroni instructed him to return to that location every year for four more years. Joseph likely had September 22nd marked on his calendar! After these yearly appointments, Joseph finally obtained the plates on September 22, 1827 (see Joseph Smith History 1:31–59).

The Details: Consider some of the following ideas to commemorate this significant date:

- Read the account regarding Moroni in the "Testimony of the Prophet Joseph Smith" at the front of The Book of Mormon.

- Talk about the principles we can learn from this account: God does answer prayers. Angels do appear. Moroni really cared about this record— he was one of the authors of the gold plates. The Book of Mormon was translated by the power of God.

- Make angel crafts, or incorporate angels in the family treat: angel food cake, angel cupcakes, angels shaped with powdered sugar on pancakes, or angel crafts.

- Watch a Church movie about Joseph receiving the plates.

- Play an alternate version of hide-and-seek. One person hides with an object representing the plates, and the others try to find that person.

- Have one family member dress in white, maybe even a white robe. Shine a bright light on them in the dark room and discuss how this is similar to or different from Joseph Smith's account as you read it.

23

THE FAMILY: A PROCLAMATION TO THE WORLD—
SEPTEMBER 23, 1995

Main Idea: Make the date of the first reading of the Family Proclamation a special day in your home. During the women's session of general conference, President Gordon B. Hinckley read the proclamation for the first time over the pulpit.

The Details: Celebrating this day could be as simple as having an extra-special breakfast or dinner and acknowledging the historic event. You may choose to focus some of your gospel study on the Proclamation. Possible activities may include the following:

- Have each person write a sentence of their choice from the Proclamation text with markers of varying colors; hang them up around the house.

- Pick a paragraph to memorize or read over multiple times.

- Share stories of extended family "lending help when needed" as the Proclamation indicates they should.

- Have family members assess how they are living the teachings of the Proclamation such as, "Happiness in family life is most likely to be achieved when founded on the teachings of the Lord Jesus Christ." Discuss how you are doing as a family in following the teachings of Jesus and how you can do better.

- Have each family member pick one principle from the sentence: "Successful marriages and families are established and maintained on principles of faith, prayer, repentance, forgiveness, respect, love, compassion, work, and wholesome recreational activities." Each person may share something your family is doing well in this area, and suggest a way your family could improve. For example, one family member could share that the family is doing a good job remembering to have family prayer together but could do better by increasing reverence and offering more thoughtful prayers.

- Plan "wholesome recreational activities" for the near future.

Tip: Since this date falls right next to the visitation of the Angel Moroni, decide in advance which Sunday in September your family can focus on the Proclamation, and plan activities that will best help family members appreciate and understand this unique document.

24

CONFERENCE CELEBRATIONS—FIRST WEEKENDS IN APRIL AND OCTOBER

Main Idea: Conference weekend can be a highlight of the year.

The Details: Possibilities for positive, fun family traditions to incorporate into this special weekend are endless. Consider whether some of the following ideas might work well for your family:

- Friday night or Saturday morning prior to the first session of conference, the children can gather in the kitchen to make some special foods, perhaps ones that you only eat on conference weekends. The foods that will work best for each family may be different; our family loves "Conference Cake" (see the following page for the recipe). A special breakfast can get everyone up and ready on time. Simple meals between sessions can also be fun and memorable. For example, one of my siblings serves egg salad sandwiches and barbeque chips because they are foods her children enjoy and they can be made ahead of time.

- Go to a unique place to watch conference. Depending on where you live, this might mean going to Grandma's house, a local Church building, a hotel, or, if possible, Temple Square. Perhaps you could watch the Saturday and Sunday sessions in different locations if it helps your children get excited or improve reverence.

- Provide "conference candy" or other small rewards for those who take notes and for those who share what they will do as a result of conference.

- Do a physical activity together like riding bikes or playing tag at the park between Saturday sessions. This helps break up sitting time and proves beneficial when children can choose the activity

- Make a tent in your living room facing the television like King Benjamin's people did when they pitched their tents towards the temple (see Mosiah 2).

- Keep your "72-hour kit" fresh by eating the food it contains—which may possibly include treats. Since conference comes every 6 months, this tradition ensures that 72- hour-kit food items stay fresh.

- Play "Conference Jeopardy" (see chapter 13).

Tip: In the weeks leading up to conference, consider doing activities to help your children review faces of the Brethren and facts about their lives; games like Concentration can be found at friend.lds.org. A little preparation beforehand can be a key factor in making general conference more meaningful.

Conference Cake
Any breakfast cake will do, but here is the Hiltons' recipe.

Ingredients for cake:
1 egg
1 cup milk
¼ cup oil
2 cups flour
¼ cup sugar
1 Tbsp. baking powder
1 tsp. salt

Ingredients for topping:
1 ½ cups packed brown sugar
1 cup flour
1 cup oats
1 ½ tsp cinnamon
⅔ cup butter or margarine, softened

Preheat oven to 400 degrees Fahrenheit. Lightly grease a 9x13 pan. For the cake, beat the egg, then stir in milk and oil. Mix in remaining ingredients just until flour is moistened (batter should be lumpy). Pour the batter in the pan, then put flour on your hands and flatten it down.

Set the cake batter aside as you prepare the topping. For the topping, mix the first four ingredients, then cut in butter until well incorporated. Sprinkle the topping on the cake batter. Bake for about 20–25 minutes until the topping is crisp.

25

JOSEPH SMITH'S BIRTHDAY—DECEMBER 23, 1805

Main Idea: Celebrate and honor Joseph Smith on or near his birthday. Fortunately, this date falls a few days before Christmas, making it easier to remember and incorporate it into our annual holiday traditions. How appropriate to remember Joseph Smith at the time of year that we are focused on the Savior. We read, "Joseph Smith . . . has done more, save Jesus only, for the salvation of men in this world, than any other man that ever lived in it" (Doctrine and Covenants 135:3).

The Details: Some activities for the day might include these:

- Read the first few pages of Joseph Smith History together.

- Draw or paint pictures of Joseph's family with names and faces of his brothers and sisters (found in Joseph Smith History 1:4). You could serve birthday treats as you retell facts or recite a scripture pertaining to Joseph.

- Act out stories from Joseph's early life, such as his leg surgery, farming, leg wrestling, or visiting different churches.

- Read and discuss Doctrine and Covenants 135.

- Music can be powerful in allowing the Holy Spirit to testify of truth. Consider singing the following hymns associated with Joseph Smith: "Joseph Smith's First Prayer" (*Hymns,* no. 26); "Praise to the Man" (*Hymns,* no. 27); or "A Poor Wayfaring Man of Grief" (*Hymns,* no. 29).

Part 3

FAMILY HISTORY SNOWBALLING

IF OUR CHILDREN MOAN WHEN we tell them we are going to do family history, perhaps we need more variety. Family history is not just searching for names. It is not just temple work. It is not just journaling. It is all of these and more. We "snowball" our children (or, in other words, we enlarge their understanding of the many facets of family history, just like a small snowball increases in size as it rolls along and gathers more snow) with family history when we engage them in a variety of activities, even activities that they might not normally associate with family history. Keep family history fresh and inviting by mixing things up a bit.

Elder Quentin L. Cook taught, "We finally have the doctrine, the temples, and the technology for families to accomplish this glorious work of salvation. I suggest one way this might be done. Families could hold a 'Family Tree Gathering.' This should be a recurring effort" ("Roots and Branches," *Ensign,* May 2014).

The activities in this section could be incorporated into a "Family Tree Gathering." You might choose to focus one Sunday a month on family history, or devote every Sunday during the entirety of a specific month. Making family history part of your Sunday routine weekly, monthly, or quarterly can help you engage in a family history snowballing.

26

INDEXING RACES

(ages 7 and up; younger children may assist and encourage)

Main Idea: Family history, and specifically indexing, is a part of your family culture that needs to be consistently nurtured. Often family members get into indexing for a while and then it falls by the wayside. If this has happened in your home, indexing races is a great way to bring this valuable service back into your family.

Materials needed: Electronic devices, a timer, and a simple reward.

- Go to http://familysearch.org/indexing and download the indexing app or program required to start indexing.

- If you have multiple children and multiple digital devices, have your children work independently to see how many names they can each index in a given period of time, like ten minutes. Children may also work in pairs with one person reading the name on the screen and the other typing it in.

- If there is only one person in the family interested in indexing, have them set a goal for how many names they think they can index in 10 minutes.

- Everyone in the family gets the reward, or gets to make a treat together if the goal is reached.

Tip: This activity works best for children over eight years old. However, to encourage involvement of younger children, consider having them be the cheerleaders, keep track of the time, count names, or offer advantages or rewards for teams that have younger players participating. It is also important to remember that accuracy is much more important than working quickly.

27

FAMILY HISTORY QUIZ CREATIONS

(ages 8 and up; younger children can participate with assistance)

Main Idea: Dust off those family history books! Help your children learn about their ancestors and find strength from their past.

Materials needed: Family history books of your ancestors, paper, and pens.

- Give each family member a book or other written material about their ancestors and invite them to spend 15 minutes creating questions about their ancestors and writing the answers to those questions. Many children can find their own questions and answers. Parents may read with children who need assistance and help them write their number of required questions (perhaps as many questions as they are years old).

- After 15 minutes, gather the papers with written questions and their answers. These become the quiz key.

- A parent can read the questions out loud and have each family member give either a written or verbal answer. The parent can then read the correct answer.

- If they desire, children may keep track of the number of questions they answer correctly.

Tip: After you put everyone's questions together, you will have a quiz that would have taken hours for one person to create. Parents will likely learn new things too! You may choose to keep these questions for future games or other activities, such as "The Magic Sunday Square" (chapter 11), "Grandparent Guesstures" (chapter 32), or "Ancestor Anniversaries and Birthdays" (chapter 31).

28

SHARING MISSION RECORDS

(all ages)

Main Idea: Rekindle the spirit of missionary work by reviewing old mission records.

Materials needed: Mission journals or records—your own or another family member's (used with permission).

Many missionaries keep a mission journal, or they have letters they wrote home or to the mission president. Unfortunately, these inspiring documents often get left in memory boxes on attic shelves. What a rewarding activity to take twenty minutes on a Sunday to read from these mission records! You might be able to read what was written on the exact same date in previous years!

This activity helps the children see what missionary life is really like. They can come to understand how companionships function, how to work with members, and what blessings come from teaching investigators. Listeners get to hear how lives are changed, prayers are answered, and how the gospel blesses lives. Additionally, the people and experiences that are near and dear to the missionary are shared with the entire family.

Perhaps the ideal time for this activity is at bedtime when the children are eager to listen to stories. Or maybe it is at mealtime when you have a captive audience. Choose whatever time works best for your family; you may get carried away for more time than was scheduled. Your mind will be filled with the sweet memories of full-time service.

Tip #1: Don't forget to show mission pictures!

Tip #2: You may come across an investigator or companion that you want to contact. Perhaps you could enlist family members to help reach out, write letters, and share their testimonies with these contacts.

Tip #3: If no one in your family or your ancestory has served a mission, you may decide to find records online.

29

JOY IN PAST JOURNEYS

(all ages)

Main Idea: Enjoy entertainment and cherish memories by viewing old family movies and photo albums. Unless you have a scheduled time to view family movies, they often are ignored and months and years go by with little or no viewing time. Children generally love to see themselves and their siblings when they were younger.

Materials needed: Old family movies and/or photo albums

The variety of ways you can do this are as numerous as the needs and stages of your family. Here are a few ideas:

- On the Sunday closest to a child's birthday, bring out video footage of their birth or footage of them as an infant and toddler.

- On the Sunday closest to your wedding anniversary, bring out your wedding video or photos.

- On the Sunday you want to devote to an ancestor (see chapter 31), share videos/photos of that ancestor's life.

- Use video footage or photo albums as an introduction for family discussions. For example, show footage of family vacations before discussing upcoming family trips, footage of family members performing before a discussion on developing talents, or a video clip of infants to introduce a discussion on the Plan of Salvation.

- If your videos are a collection of experiences, just turn them on to enjoy together. When a scene connected to a doctrine or principle is shown, pause the movie for a minute to share a testimony of that doctrine. This is definitely an activity to delight in!

30

FOCUS ON FACES

(ages 3 and up, depending on the version played)

Main Idea: Knowing stories, knowing names, and knowing family lines are all fantastic, but there is a different feeling that comes from knowing ancestors' faces. While knowing their faces is not essential to submitting names for the temple, it is beneficial if we want to feel personal and close to them. Using methods similar to the game "Memory" or "Concentration," match faces with names, or put pictures in correct family lines. These games will help family members focus on the faces of your ancestors.

Materials needed: Photos of your ancestors. The number of photos could be anywhere between 6–100, depending on how challenging you want the game to be.

Gather photos of your ancestors from actual photo albums, digital albums, and online searches. Familysearch.org can house photos of all your ancestors and may have more photos than your family has seen. Once you have gathered pictures of your ancestors, get ready to play a game that will involve and challenge the entire family.

- *Focus on Faces Level One—Concentration with photos only.* For the easiest version, print two copies of the photos and play a simple matching game. Lay all the photos facedown in a random order. One player begins by turning over two cards and putting them back facedown in the same space they were previously. Then the next player chooses two cards. When a match is found, the player can keep the matched pair and take one additional turn revealing two cards. Play continues until all the pairs are found.

- *Focus on Faces Level Two—Concentration with names and photos.* Print one copy of the photos. On another card write the names of the ancestors pictured. Play the matching game as above, pairing the name with the correct photo.

- *Focus on Faces Level Three—Photo family tree*. As in *Focus on Faces Level Two*, prepare one set of photos and one set of name cards. Using the photo and name cards, see if you can create the family tree with the faces and names in the right places.

- *Focus on Faces Level Four—Photo family tree using photos only*. Lay out a photo family tree on the floor or table using photos only. There may be empty spaces if photos are missing. To make it possible to complete the tree, you might have a family member do their best drawing of the ancestors whose photos are missing.

Tip #1: The biggest hurdle to playing this game is locating the photos. One solution is to put children in charge of finding, printing, and cutting out the photos. This can be half the fun. Depending on the age of the child, they may need help finding the first photo. Then stand back and let them enjoy discovering more on their own.

31

ANCESTOR ANNIVERSARIES AND BIRTHDAYS
(all ages)

Main Idea: One of the most joyous parts of family history is really coming to know your ancestors in greater depth. To encourage this, remember and honor ancestors on the Sunday nearest their wedding anniversary or birthday. Gather information on one individual, and give them their own day of honor.

Materials needed: Facts about chosen ancestor; additional materials will depend on which of the following activities are chosen.

Depending on how fresh the details of the honored ancestor are in your mind, this Sunday activity might take more than a few minutes of preparation. You may want to share this responsibility with all family members—keep in mind that the more a family member participates as an active learner, the more they will remember. Consider the following activities:

- Share basic facts about this individual, or better yet, have your children share them! This could include answers to the following questions: Where and when were they born? How did they receive their name? What were their parents' names? What was their occupation? What was one of their childhood experiences? What characteristics distinguished them? What teachings/sayings are they known for?"

- Prepare their favorite meal or favorite treat. Eat as you share the facts about their life. Keep it simple.

- Show photos of the ancestor or video recordings if they are available.

- Share inspirational stories about the ancestor. Children can tell or act out the stories themselves, which will help them internalize the positive character traits of their ancestors.

- Play simple games your ancestor might have played.

- Make a paper chain (or other type of material) and read and discuss the counsel from President Hinckley: "We are the beneficiaries of the visions and the dreams, the labors and the sacrifices of all who have gone before us. They are gone, and we are here. . . . Never become a weak link in the chain of your family's generations" ("Keep the Chain Unbroken," BYU Devotional, 30 November 1999).

Tip: Personalize the activities around what is unique to the particular ancestor being remembered. For example, my grandpa is known as someone who served missions to South America, enjoyed hiking, told jokes, and loved to laugh. For activities to honor and remember him we might read some of his mission records, learn phrases in Spanish, or eat South American food. One child could prepare a few jokes to tell.

32

GRANDPARENT GUESSTURES

(all ages)

Main Idea: Play a game of fast-moving charades in which all the skits and stories come from ancestors' lives.

Materials needed: A timer and slips of paper with brief descriptions depicting a family history event or story.

Instructions:

- Brainstorm a list of phrases describing experiences in grandparents' and great-grandparents' lives. It may take a few minutes of preparation for you and your children to come up with a list. Limit the descriptions to one sentence. Type up the list and save it so you can easily add to it the next time you play. (You may choose to save it at http://familysearch.org as well.)

- Place the one-line descriptions in a bowl or other container.

- Gather the family together and decide if you will split into teams or play non-competitively as a whole group. Because many scenes are easier to act out with at least two people, you might choose to have two people on the same team act out a scene together.

- Set a timer for two minutes. Have one person at a time choose a slip of paper and begin acting out the scene or story written on the slip of paper. Once someone guesses the correct scenario by naming what scene from your family history is being acted out AND the name of the ancestor involved, the actor can then select another slip of paper and begin acting out the next scenario. They may continue this until the time is up.

- The team is awarded the amount of points equal to the scenes guessed correctly during the allotted time. An additional point is awarded if someone on the team can say how they are related to the featured ancestor in each experience that was acted out.

- Play continues with someone from the other team choosing slips of paper and acting out as many scenarios as possible in two minutes. Then round two begins with the first team acting as before.

Note: Each family's specific list of events will be particular to their own ancestry. Here is a sample list from our Grandparent Guesstures:

- A great-grandmother crawling on her hands and knees when her feet were too frozen to continue her handcart journey.

- A great-grandmother telling her family that she believed the restored gospel and was going to cross the plains without them (she succeeded!).

- A grandmother playing the piano for income at a popular town dance.

- A grandfather in front of the kitchen sink in a farmhouse, proposing to his future wife.

- A grandfather as a young boy setting up traps to catch animals.

- A grandfather throwing members of a mob down the stairway when they threatened his life.

Tip #1: After playing this multiple times, and family members have become very familiar with the scenes and experiences, you may choose to make "Grandparent Guesstures" more challenging by offering additional points if the team can name more details about the scene. For example: an additional point for when it happened, where it happened, and naming others who may have also been involved in the scene.

33
WHEN I WAS YOUNG
(all ages)

Main Idea: Take the opportunity to share journal accounts from younger days. Reading accounts from days past can be an enlightening and joyful experience for the whole family.

The Details: Consider some of the following ideas:

- Gather the children around the couch or around the dinner table and read your journal out loud to them. (Feel free to edit if necessary!) You could share entries from your life that coincide with the ages of your children. If parents did not keep journals when they were young, draw on journals of grandparents or aunts and uncles (if available and with permission).

- Turn to the same month and day from a previous year in your journal and read the entry from that day.

- Read a Sunday entry and learn what you did on Sundays as a youth.

- Read journal entries as a bedtime story.

- Expand on the stories that you read, and talk about your feelings when you were younger.

- Select ahead of time specific important events from your journal that you would like to share with your children.

- Invite older children who have kept journals to read their entries from years past.

Personal Note: This activity has been very beneficial for me. As I read my journal to my children, it helps me remember experiences I had as a child, which in turn helps me better understand my children. We've read that

I missed days practicing the piano and even stayed up past my bedtime (why would I do that?). I've realized I can't be too upset at my children when they do the same things—they're just like me!

34

FAMILY HISTORY LIVE RECORDINGS
(all ages)

Main Idea: Bring family history alive by having your children interview their parents, grandparents, aunts, uncles, brothers, and sisters. Recording devices are easy to access on phones and tablets so it can take little effort to record priceless memories and information. Draw on some of the following ideas as you create audiovisual family history records.

Materials needed: Paper and writing utensils for note taking, recording devices. Computer and editing software, if available, but they are not mandatory for this activity.

Choose any one of the following ideas as you create audiovisual family history records.

- Locate at http://familysearch.org a list of 52 questions to ask family members about their lives. Children could use these questions to interview immediate or extended family members. For example, they might ask: How did you get your name? What is one of your favorite holiday memories? Tell me about your brothers and sisters and memories you have with them? What was a favorite family vacation? How did you choose your occupation?

- Use already scheduled family gatherings. Extended families who live close by each other may regularly gather together on a Sunday. A few minutes of these gatherings could conveniently be turned into meaningful interviews and storytelling. If you don't live near family, video conference calls could also be recorded.

- Take the opportunity to record your own children. Occasionally, perhaps monthly, record each family member talking for a few minutes about their current interests. Older children may be able to use video editing software to help splice together clips across time.

Tip #1: Bedtime can be a convenient moment to generate family history. You could answer some of the 52 questions from http://familysearch.org as your children lie in bed, and record yourself telling these stories. Great stories for the kids and family history created—a double blessing! And if the grandparents happen to be over, they can put the kids to bed—a triple blessing!

Tip #2: Once you have recorded your interview, upload it to http://familysearch.org. This will ensure it won't disappear and will be easily accessible to others.

35

JUMP TO JOURNALING

(all ages)

Main Idea: Blessings come to those who keep a journal. Take a few minutes on Sunday to help your children record experiences that are happening to them.

Materials needed: Hardbound journals and pens for each family member or digital devices if digital journals are preferred.

President Henry B. Eyring shared,

> When our children were very small, I started to write down a few things about what happened every day. . . . I never missed a day no matter how tired I was or how early I would have to start the next day. Before I would write, I would ponder this question: "Have I seen the hand of God reaching out to touch us or our children or our family today?" As I kept at it, something began to happen. As I would cast my mind over the day, I would see evidence of what God had done for one of us that I had not recognized in the busy moments of the day. As that happened, and it happened often, I realized that trying to remember had allowed God to show me what He had done. ("O Remember, Remember," *Ensign*, November 2007)

Getting children started writing journal entries can be a challenge, but it can end up being a memorable Sabbath activity. Young children participate by drawing a picture in a journal and then having an older sibling write the child's explanation of the drawing. Length and detail are not as important as the habit that is forming and the process of thinking and writing about their lives. Often the simple things will be the most intriguing later on.

Everyone has something to write! It may be helpful to give your children prompts. Nephi recorded both spiritual experiences and other events from daily life. We learn from both types of entries. For example, you could ask your children to write experiences based on the following prompts:

- Write a story about when the Lord answered your prayers.

- When have you followed a prompting from the Holy Ghost?

- When was a time that you found comfort from a scripture?

- Tell a story about when you served somebody and how it made you feel.

- Write about your memories of your baptism and confirmation.

You could also ask simple questions like:

- What has been your favorite vacation?

- What are your hobbies?

- Who are your friends?

- What games do you like to play?

Tip #1: Sunday is also prime time for parents to briefly journal about children. Write down fun things children said during the week, or ask young children what they want you to record about them. You might choose one Sunday of the month to write a summary of that month. At the end of the year, you can compile each monthly summary for a yearly history.

Tip#2: If children are recording more meaningful events, they can record them in their personal journal and also type them into familysearch.org to ensure their posterity has a copy. Wouldn't you love to read fresh details about an ancestor's baptism day or their answers to prayers?

A promise from a prophet: "People often use the excuse that their lives are uneventful and nobody would be interested in what they have done. But I promise you that if you will keep your journals and records, they will indeed be a source of great inspiration to your families, to your children, your grandchildren, and others, on through the generations" (Spencer W. Kimball, "President Kimball Speaks Out on Personal Journals," *Ensign*, December 1980).

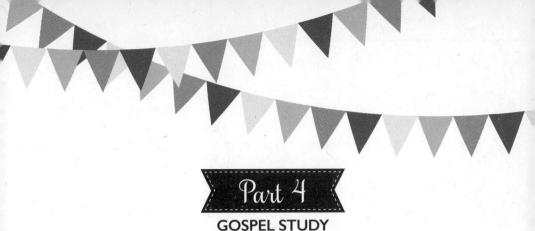

Part 4

GOSPEL STUDY

GOSPEL STUDY AND INSTRUCTION IS one of four activities the First Presidency asked parents to give highest priority to in the letter quoted in the introduction to this book. Their quote bears repeating here: "We counsel parents and children to give highest priority to family prayer, family home evening, *gospel study and instruction*, and wholesome family activities. However worthy and appropriate other demands or activities may be, they must not be permitted to displace the divinely-appointed duties that only parents and families can adequately perform" ("Letter from the First Presidency," February 11, 1999; emphasis added). Although gospel study and instruction can and should take place during the week, I believe there is a special spirit and power that accompanies gospel learning on the Sabbath day.

Gospel study isn't always fun and games. Often it means sitting down and doing some serious study. This can pose challenges and potentially create an environment where some children don't want to participate. Even though my siblings and I behaved like normal (and sometimes a bit difficult) children while growing up in our parents' home, I am grateful my father and mother persisted and engaged our family in meaningful gospel study. Perfect scenarios are not required for the Spirit to be present and the gospel to be taught. Children may be more eager participants than you might initially expect.

Remember, the setting of the lesson makes a difference. It can be helpful to change locations from time to time. Perhaps gospel games are played in the family room, but a Sunday lesson might be taught around the kitchen table where family members can have better access to paper, pen, and scriptures.

Gospel study does not need to be long and it definitely doesn't need to be boring. It can become an important part of our Sunday worship and help our children become more familiar with the teachings of Jesus Christ.

36

EXPLORE THE SOURCES

(all ages; tailor the source to fit the age)

Main Idea: Help your children explore the wonderful Church resources that are available.

Materials needed: A variety of Church materials like illustrated scripture stories, current or old issues of Church magazines, *Behold Your Little Ones* nursery manual, Primary manuals, *Come Follow Me* manuals, *Teachings of the Presidents of the Church* manuals, *True to the Faith*, and other scripture books (see the Gospel Library app). You can also utilize online websites like lds.org, friend.lds.org, newera.lds.org, or mormon.org. Choose one of the ideas below that best suits your family on any given week.

- Gather the children around. Set out as many of the above gospel resources as you can find. Invite them to pick any resource. Depending on how much time you have, give them anywhere from 10–30 minutes to explore the source they chose. Ask them to be prepared to share what they learned with the whole family when you gather back after the designated time period. Giving the children a choice of what they study makes them feel more ownership. Once the time is up, let your children teach each other what they learned, either in pairs or sharing one at a time in front of everyone.

- Choose four different gospel resources and place them in four separate areas of the room. Have individual family members rotate to each area for 10–15 minutes at a time; for example, you might set it up so that everyone gets 15 minutes of Church magazines, 15 minutes of scriptures stories, 15 minutes of Bible Videos, and 15 minutes of Mormon Messages. Choose and arrange these resources as you feel best fits the interests and needs of your family.

- Assign children to prepare a three-minute talk on different gospel top-ics. Turn everyone loose for 10 minutes to prepare, then meet back together to hear the prepared talks. Instruct family members that each talk should inclue a personal example, a quote from the source they chose, and a scripture. "True to the Faith" and the "Gospel Principles" manual are a good resource for this activity.

- Children who love to be online may explore sources like Church web-sites. There is a wealth of content on lds.org, such that we couldn't explore it all even if we devoted months of Sundays. Family members may watch videos or read articles, depending on their interest, and then report on what they watched or read.

Online favorites for your children may include:

- http://scriptures.lds.org (watch three-minute video clips)

- http://Mormonmessages.org

- http://BibleVideos.org

- http://Mormonchannel.org or the mormon channel app for mobile devises (audio and video programs usually 30 minutes in length)

- http://friend.lds.org (print coloring pages, read articles, play learning games)

- http://newera.lds.org and youth.lds.org (videos, article and music)

- http://mormon.org

Tip #1: Many programs on mormonchannel.org like *Gospel Solutions for Families*, *Conversations*, and *Here to Help*, are likely appropriate for the entire family. These programs are wonderful to hear during meal preparation time or while getting ready for church. To encourage more attentive listening, tell family members you will play "Magic Sunday Square" with teachings from the episode.

Tip #2: Children often love having their entire family's attention when giving reports or talks. Allowing children to teach on their own may just be the most fun and memorable for them.

37

PRESENTING *PREACH MY GOSPEL*

(ages 7 and up)

Main Idea: *Preach My Gospel* is a one-of-a-kind manual containing its own instructions, study tips, and lesson material. "Our own study of *Preach My Gospel* will not only help us to develop a greater understanding and appreciation for our missionaries, but it will help us in our own day-to-day life. Every member of our family owns a copy of *Preach My Gospel*. Studying this guide is a great support in developing a strong testimony. It helps us understand fundamental gospel principles and the desire to serve" (Erich W. Kopischke, "Preach My Gospel—the Unifying Tool between Members and Missionaries" *Ensign*, Nov 2007).

As you study *Preach my Gospel* together you will discuss fundamental gospel principles and turn to vital scriptures. This is a powerful tool for future missionaries, and the best MTC is the home. Elder Scott taught this clearly when he said, "I encourage you to find out how this extraordinary resource [*Preach My Gospel*] can help in your missionary efforts . . . as a parent preparing a child for a mission" (Elder Richard G. Scott, "The Power of Preach my Gospel," *Ensign*, May 2005). The power in *Preach My Gospel* can be felt only if we take the time to read and study its contents.

The Details: Materials needed: copies of *Preach My Gospel* for each family member, printed or digital, pens and paper, scriptures.

Consider starting as a family with the "First Presidency Message" and the "Introduction." Then you may feel inspired to have your children look at the "Table of Contents" and choose which chapters they feel are immediately applicable to their lives. If you have a child learning a foreign language, he might like to start with chapter 10. If a child is struggling to study the scriptures effectively, she might like to begin start with chapter 2.

If family members need to do better at using time wisely, they might be interested in starting with chapter 8.

As you study, remember the purpose is to go slowly and really digest the material. You may take a year to go through the entire manual, spending roughly a month on each chapter, reading word for word, section by section. You may decide to take turns reading sections, or have each person read one paragraph aloud. When you come to the scripture study sections, look up the scripture references. Do the suggested activities under the "Activity" headings. It is effective study, not the amount covered, that facilitates learning.

Some specific suggestions to consider include the following:

- Chapter 2 ("How Do I Study Effectively and Prepare to Teach?") is very applicable to family members. Take time to think about the items listed under "Consider This" and "Remember This." Under the "Study and Application" section, tailor the suggestions to fit your children's roles: Instead of "I think about the people I am teaching when I study" they could change the phrase to "I think about the people I can influence," or "I think about the challenges I am facing when I study."

- Chapter 3 ("What Do I Study and Teach?") offers concrete study and teaching ideas. Depending on the age of your children, you may want to teach your children the doctrine; or, if they are capable, this is a perfect opportunity to let your children practice the teaching tips on each other.

- Chapter 6 ("How Do I Develop Christlike Attributes?") dives into essential characteristics that will immensely bless your family. Clear language and probing questions allow each child to assess how he or she is currently doing in the quest to be like the Savior.

- Chapter 8 ("How Do I Use Time Wisely?") provides excellent time management and goal setting tips! Don't be deterred by the mission reports and other mission-related charts. You may want to quickly overview those pages and focus instead on the daily planning sheet that is appropriate for all age groups. Let family members take the time to create their own daily planning sheet or print one they like from online instead. They can see how managing time, regardless of their age, brings blessings.

Studying *Preach My Gospel* takes time and effort; however, as a result your family will likely be more focused and prepared as servants of God. Ask for their ideas for what to focus on the next time through. The needs of family members will have changed and they may be more proficient learners.

Tip: You or your children may prefer to use the compact 6-inch size, which includes everything the larger size contains but may seem less daunting (and is less expensive).

38

MIRACULOUS MUSIC

(all ages)

Main Idea: Spiritual strength is found in the hymns! The First Presidency has said, "Music has boundless powers for moving families toward greater spirituality and devotion to the gospel. Latter-day Saints should fill their homes with the sound of worthy music. Ours is a hymnbook for the home as well as for the meetinghouse. We hope the hymnbook will take a prominent place among the scriptures and other religious books in our homes" ("First Presidency Preface," *Hymns*, x).

Teach your children to love the hymns by singing them! Have the spirit of the Primary songs and hymns pervade your home, especially on the Sabbath.

Materials needed: LDS *Hymns* and *Children's Songbook,* printed or digital, and other uplifting music.

Set the mood for the Sabbath by playing background music throughout the day, especially first thing in the morning. In addition, here are other music ideas to consider:

- Have "Sunday Music Time." If you have children who play a musical instrument, they could perform hymns they are learning, with the family singing along.

- Choose one hymn and sing it every Sunday during the month to really learn it well. You may focus on a different verse each week.

- Play "name that tune" with hymns or Primary songs.

- Play a type of musical Pictionary by having everyone illustrate a hymn and then guess what Church hymn each person illustrated.

- Illustrate one hymn together by having each family member choose one line to portray through some form of art, drawing, clipart, or paint.

- Explore Church websites and let your children choose songs they want to hear.

- Play musical charades by having family members act out the title of hymns or Primary songs.

- If children have musical experience, consider inviting them to *create* some gospel music.

In addition to the hymns and Primary songs, numerous websites offer free and/or continuous music:

- https://www.lds.org/youth/music contains dozens of free upbeat and slower reverent songs that can inspire children, youth, and adults.

- https://www.lds.org/general-conference/music?lang=eng contains numerous music recordings from general conference.

- https://www.lds.org/callings/primary/leader-resources/music or the Church music app provides the option of listening to Primary songs, with or without the lyrics and in other languages. On the music website, there is also an option for listening to only soprano, alto, tenor, or bass parts—an excellent option for little singers.

- Find hundreds of uplifting music videos on YouTube and other sites by searching "lds music." These can include sing-along karaoke videos for children made by the Church or Church members.

- Use resources at http://friend.lds.org, which include simplified arrangements for the beginning pianist and music that has been printed in the *Friend* magazine but is not printed in the *Children's Songbook*. Both audio recordings and sheet music are available for download. You will find songs like "Scripture Power," "The Family Is of God," and "I Know That My Savior Loves Me." All are beautiful songs, especially for the Sabbath!

If you don't know the hymns and primary songs well enough, begin now to learn. If cooperation is lacking, offer rewards or simply play background music throughout the day. Fill your home with worthy music and feel the spirit of your home change with the push of a button!

39

PROGRESS WITH PROGRAMS

(all ages, but geared to 8 and older)

Main Idea: Depending on the age and gender of your children, help them work on *Faith in God, Personal Progress,* or *Duty to God.*

The Details: The First Presidency said to children around the world, "Earning the Faith in God Award will help you become the kind of person you would like to be and the person Heavenly Father knows you can become" ("Message from the First Presidency," *Faith in God*).

Speaking of programs for youth, President Henry B. Eyring said:

> You know of two powerful programs provided by the Lord.
> One, for young women, is called Personal Progress. The
> other, for Aaronic Priesthood holders, is called Duty to
> God. We encourage young people in the rising generation
> to see their own potential to build great spiritual strength.
> And we plead with those who care about those young
> people to rise to what the Lord requires of us to help
> them. . . . [The] contents of these booklets are a physical
> representation of the Lord's trust in the rising generation
> and in all of us who love them. ("Help Them on Their
> Way Home," *Ensign*, May 2010)

By sharing these quotations and similar counsel from Church leaders, we can help children realize that these programs are not checklists; rather they are guideposts to increase their spiritual power in these latter days. Consider some of the requirements from these booklets that one could easily help children do on a Sunday afternoon:

- "Mark these verses about the Holy Ghost in your scriptures: John 14:16–17, 2 Nephi 32:5, and Moroni 10:5. Discuss ways the Holy

Ghost helps you" ("Learning and Living the Gospel," *Faith in God for Girls*, 2003).

- "Write a poem, story, or short play that teaches a principle of the gospel or is about Heavenly Father's creations" ("Developing Talents," *Faith in God for Boys,* 2003).

- "Look up the word *integrity* in a dictionary. Interview your mother, grandmother, or another woman you respect about her understanding and application of the word. Make a list of ways you can make your actions consistent with your knowledge of right and wrong, and record in your journal what it means to you to have integrity" ("Integrity," *Young Women Personal Progress*, 2009).

- "Think about your personal prayers. How often do you pray? How do you feel when you pray? Study James 1:5–6; Alma 34:17–28; 3 Nephi 18:15–21; and Moroni 10:3–5. Identify principles that can help make your prayers more meaningful and the blessings that will come as you 'pray always'" ("Spiritual Strength," *Fulfilling My Duty to God*, 2009).

During the week, talk with Primary and/or Young Women and Young Men leaders about what they are hoping your children will do with the *Faith in God, Personal Progress,* or *Duty to God* programs. Act on their suggestions, or share their suggestion with your children as you simply sit down with them and let them choose what they could work on to participate in these programs. Often, it is appropriate and helpful to involve other family members in doing these requirements, even if they are not in the age group or gender specified in the particular program. Even five-year-olds like to learn how to lead a song, participate in a play, or interview a family member.

40

REPORTING LIVE FROM *FOR THE STRENGTH OF YOUTH*
(ages 7 and up)

Main Idea: One of the most powerful documents to guide families is *For the Strength of Youth* (*FSY*). Speaking to young people, President Dieter F. Uchtdorf taught: "Some of the most important guidelines for your life are found in the pamphlet *For the Strength of Youth*. . . . [T]he doctrine and principles it presents are an invaluable treasure. You . . . who are already 18 or older, if you don't have this booklet anymore, make sure to get one, keep it, and use it. This little booklet is a gem for any age group. It contains standards which are sacred symbols representing our membership in the Church" ("See the End from the Beginning," *Ensign*, May 2006).

For this activity, family members take the job of a newspaper reporter who reports about the "Who, What, When, Where, Why, and How" of a standard from *For the Strength of Youth*.

Materials needed: *For the Strength of Youth* booklet, recording device, and editing software or apps (if desired).

Invite each of your children to pick a chapter from *For the Strength of Youth* and carefully read it. Encourage them to mark specific phrases that stand out to them and to read the scriptures listed in the pamphlet. They could also include a "role play" in the report.

Give a recording device (e.g., phone, tablet, etc.) to each family member and ask them to prepare a 1–2-minute newscast that summarizes the "Who, What, When, Where, Why, and How" of the standard they selected. The "Who" and "When" will be obvious (All of us! Right now!) but the others will be different. For example, consider this report that could be given based on the standard, "Entertainment and the Media."

"Hi, this is Rebekah, reporting live from FSY news, bringing you an important update today on the standard, 'Entertainment and the Media.' You know that this involves YOU, and this is something that affects our lives NOW. Why is this such a big issue? According to *For the Strength of Youth*, '[W]hatever you read, listen to, or look at influences you. Select only media that uplifts you.' That means this is important!

"You might be wondering, 'What should I do if I encounter bad media?' The *FSY* answer is clear: 'Have the courage to walk out of a movie, change your music, or turn off a computer, television, or mobile device if what you see or hear drives away the Spirit.'

"Keep in mind, all media isn't bad. *For the Strength of Youth* says, 'The information and entertainment provided through these media can increase your ability to learn, communicate, and become a force for good in the world.' So, go out there and do some good! I'm Rebekah, reporting live from FSY."

True entertainment is found in children recording themselves and then watching each other's "broadcasts." Get a few copies of the *For the Strength of Youth* for your children to mark. *FSY* booklets are free from Church Distribution or your ward leaders. The website http://youth.lds.org also provides short videos and articles that correlate with the FSY topics.

Tip: If *For the Strength of Youth* seems too challenging for small children, try the same activity with *My Gospel Standards*, which is part of the Primary curriculum. Let your children unleash their creativity as they teach each other about the standards.

41

AMAZING MEMORIZING

(ages 3 and older)

Main Idea: A spiritual power comes into our lives as we memorize scripture. Multiple prophets, seers, and revelators have encouraged us to do this.

Elder Richard G. Scott taught: "Great power can come from memorizing scriptures. To memorize a scripture is to forge a new friendship. It is like discovering a new individual who can help in time of need, give inspiration and comfort, and be a source of motivation for needed change ("The Power of Scripture," *Ensign*, November 2011).

The Details: Sunday is the perfect time to memorize scriptures. Consider the following ideas for how this can be done:

- Have children write out a scripture on poster board or a large piece of paper. Recite the verse or phrase a few times on Sunday and then at breakfast during the week. Erase one word at a time and continue reciting.

- Write down the first letter of each word as a review to see if you can remember all the words of the verse—this is a favorite and effective tool, especially for longer passages (see *Teaching, No Greater Call* [The Church of Jesus Christ of Latter-day Saints], Section F, "Methods of Teaching").

- A child can create motions that go along with the words; do the actions each time you recite the verse.

- Set the words of a scripture to music.

- Download the app "LDS Doctrinal Mastery" (free on Android and iOS devices). Upload a verse or section from your gospel library (scriptures, Family Proclamation, The Living Christ, or another part of the gospel library app) to the "LDS Doctrinal Mastery" app. The app takes away one word at a time, shows first letters of words, and offers matching games and other aids in memorization.

- Practice a verse you've already started learning by printing out a copy and cutting the words into different strips so that you have a jumble of words or phrases. Have children time themselves putting the word strips together in the correct order as fast as they can. Let them repeat and beat their best time.

- Perhaps Sunday could be the day to "pass off" the scripture from the previous Sunday, or one you have been learning throughout the week.

Tip #1: If a child feels too much pressure or if it causes undue stress to memorize word for word, consider reviewing Elder Devin G. Durrant's counsel about "ponderizing" (see "My Heart Pondereth Continually," *Ensign*, November 2015).

Tip #2: Preschool-age children are often capable of memorizing complete scriptures and even longer verses one phrase at a time.

Personal Note: A young person I'll call Alejandra shared an experience that helped me understand the power of memorizing scriptures. As a seminary student, she memorized the doctrinal mastery verses. When she went to college, most of her friends did not share her standards and they frequently invited her to participate in activities that were not appropriate. Normally Alejandra declined, but one evening she was feeling particularly lonely. "Maybe it wouldn't hurt to go with them one time," she thought. As she was trying to decide whether she should go, the words from a doctrinal mastery verse came to her mind. That helped her decide not to go.

That night, Alejandra's friends were involved in drinking alcohol and driving. A terrible accident occurred, and they were all killed. This dramatic story shows how memorizing a scripture can literally save a life.

42

GOSPEL ART

(all ages)

Main Idea: Art is a unique way to draw closer to the Lord and learn of Him. There are numerous beautiful ways to use art for this purpose. These include learning from the gospel art pictures, viewing artistic masterpieces, or even creating your own art.

The Details: Consider any of the following ideas that will be best for your family.

- Learn or review scripture stories with the *Gospel Art Book*. It is an inexpensive book produced by the Church (2009) that contains over 100 pictures and is accessible on the gospel library app and is online for free (https://www.lds.org/bc/content/shared/content/english/pdf/language-materials/06048_eng.pdf?lang=eng). Children seem to pay better attention and remember details when a picture is shown as you talk about the scripture story depicted. Challenge older family members to put the "Gospel Art" pictures in chronological order, organize them according to the book of scripture in which they are found, or discuss ways they might depict the story differently than the artist has portrayed it.

- Look at masterpieces of Christian art. You could select specific ones or have your children search for their own online. Each family member could select a piece of art, learn about what it depicts, and share with family members what they learned. For example, one favorite piece of art is "The Last Supper" by Leonardo da Vinci. A child could be assigned to study that painting along with reading Mark 14:22–31 (don't forget the JST, Mark 14:20–26!) and share with the family what he learned about the Last Supper.

- Create art with crayons, watercolors, coloring pages, playdough, or clay. Children could draw a temple, paint a picture of the Savior, or color Bible stories. Playdough sculptures of the tree of life, Mt. Sinai, or Noah's ark can also be Sunday appropriate.

- Use computer programs to create digital artwork. One young person found several verses about the Savior and then used a computer program to change the color of different verses so that the resulting image looked like a picture of the Savior—it was incredible! She framed her work so that it could be a constant reminder of what the Savior meant to her.

Select a method that will help your family engage with gospel art on the Sabbath day. Whether it's having your oldest child teach the younger children from the *Gospel Art Book* or breaking out the watercolors for everybody to paint a masterpiece, you'll want to give it a try!

43
POWER FROM PROPHETS
(ages 7 and up)

Main Idea: Spend time focusing on talks from the most recent general conference.

Materials needed: Digital or hard copies of conference talks, half sheets of paper, writing utensils, and a whiteboard or chalkboard.

Consider the following ideas:

- Have "pancakes with the prophets" or "conference crepes" and informally discuss one conference talk over a delicious breakfast or lunch!

- Provide a quiet ten minutes while each family member silently reads a speaker's talk, and then shares their favorite part. When family members report on talks, you may find success when four "P"s are used: **Pick** a conference talk to read and report. Allowing each child to select which talk they want to read (or listen to) helps them feel more invested in the talk. **Present** favorite parts of talks to the rest of the family, which will help them solidify what they have learned. **Post** a favorite sentence or phrase on the whiteboard or chalkboard so that everyone can remember a key part of the talk. **Plan** something to do differently because of what is taught; use the half sheets to record the plans made. The greatest power comes when we apply what we have learned and felt. The plan to do something different can be an individual goal or a family goal.

- If possible, give each family member their own copy of the conference issue labeled with their name. Keep the issues in a central place so they are always available when it is time to use them as a family. Depending on your family's preferences, digital copies may be the best option.

- If external motivation is needed, have one person read the talk aloud and afterwards play one of the gospel games to bring in a little fun. For example, in The Magic Sunday Square (see chapter 11) players can answer questions like, "President Monson talked about God's love for us and that it never changes. True or False." For the Scripture Sports (see chapter 12), players would need to turn to the correct talk in their own conference issue from which a particular quote was taken. Alternately, if you are focusing on one talk, players may find the location of a quote in that talk.

- Play Conference Jeopardy! (see chapter 13) to review talks from conference and involve all members of the family.

Counsel from general conference can be the most applicable scriptural teaching for the whole family. Sunday offers prime time to dive into prophetic preaching.

44

STORIES OF JESUS

(all ages)

Main Idea: Read short accounts from the Savior's life and discuss principles from the storyline. Since there are so many other books of scripture and places to go for gospel study, it is refreshing to simply focus on the stories of Jesus.

Materials needed: The scriptures, especially the four Gospels in the New Testament and the book of 3rd Nephi in the Book of Mormon.

On a day that is set apart to focus on the Savior, it is very appropriate to refresh our knowledge of the events of His life, His interactions with others, and His teachings. Simply open any of the four Gospels and begin reading. Frequently, one storyline will only be a few verses long, so it's possible to review multiple experiences in a short period of time.

To allow children to have a say in what you study, you could have them choose which Gospel: Matthew, Mark, Luke, or John. Then have them choose a random number. Their chosen number corresponds to the chapter you will turn to. If they choose the Gospel of Mark, they pick a number between 1–16; Matthew, 1–28; Luke, 1–24; and John, 1–21. Turn to that chapter and begin reading anywhere in the chapter. You may find it helpful to pause after every few verses to summarize or put things in your own words.

- You may turn to John 5 and read about Jesus healing a man on the Sabbath, or teaching about taking the gospel to the dead.

- You could turn to Luke 18 and read the parable of the unjust judge, and how Jesus invited the little children to come unto Him.

- Perhaps you will turn to Mark 7 and read how Jesus cast the devil out of a girl and healed a deaf man.

- In the book of 3rd Nephi, chapters 10–28 also contain the Savior's words, interactions, and teachings. Read a few verses anywhere in these chapters and feel of the Savior's love and simple doctrine.

It is up to you how far you read, what kind of detailed explanation you decide to use or not use, and how long you continue. Even simply reading from the scriptural accounts brings a beautiful spirit and increases knowledge of the Savior's dealings among people He loved. Remember, you don't need to read the whole chapter, and you can skip parts and focus on specific or favorite sections. Fortunately, you can never go wrong with accounts of Jesus.

Tip #1: For younger children, you may choose to read to them from the illustrated *New Testament Stories* (LDS edition) or have them watch short video clips from the life of Jesus found on scriptures.lds.org or BibleVideos.lds.org. Then choose one to act out or learn more about.

Tip #2: Children love to dress up or perform. Acting out the miracles Jesus performed, with or without simple costumes, can be a good way for them to remember and internalize them.

45

FAMILY COUNCIL WITHOUT THE FAMILY FEUD

(all ages)

Main Idea: Sunday is a great day for family council. Turn this into a positive experience for everyone by remembering the underlying purposes: to teach, train, and express love.

The Details: The following ideas have come from families who have found success in their family councils:

- Have family members write down concerns/compliments during the week and place them in a family council jar. This helps the emotion that might have erupted during the week have time to cool before the discussion on Sunday.

- Implement a rule that anyone who brings up a problem needs to bring two possible solutions.

- Have some ground rules that teach your family how to successfully counsel together: Everyone's voice is important, but parents are in charge of the discussion and make the final decisions and rules. Everyone will have the opportunity to speak before any decision is made, as long as they are speaking respectfully.

- Remember the family council doesn't require the entire family meeting together. Breaking into smaller groups can offer a more peaceful situation. Elder and Sister Ballard taught, "It may be just one child with a father or mother, but it can be a very important family council. You don't have to have everyone sitting together in order to have a family council" ("Family Councils: A Conversation with Elder and Sister Ballard," *Ensign*, June 2003).

Additionally, Elder Ballard shared,

> A council is when parents let their children help solve the problem. And when everyone agrees to a solution, everyone will have ownership of the problem. If I tell the family, "You go out and pull the weeds," there may be complaining or hurt feelings. But if I can help them to feel, "We all decided this," then the family council is truly working. Before you know it, family members will be organizing themselves, saying, "You do this and I'll do that." That's the power of a council. . . . My feeling is that the more fluid, the more nonthreatening, the more natural a family council is, the more effective it is. ("Family Councils: A Conversation with Elder and Sister Ballard," *Ensign,* June 2003)

Consider some additional elements of a family council that you may implement:

Committees: Councils also may include breaking off into assigned groups or committees to discuss topics such as planning the next family trip, the next birthday celebration, family menus, and assignment of family chores. Parents may need to be involved in the committee goals and direction, but sharing responsibility eliminates the problem of one family member (possibly an older sibling) from dominating decisions.

Calendaring: Sunday can be an ideal day for calendaring, coordinating everyone's schedule for the upcoming week. The older your children get, the more complicated but vital this activity becomes. One family with multiple teenagers has each child enter their activities in a specific color on Google Calendars. Then they come together to discuss conflicts or concerns. We have found that effective coordination and scheduling on Sunday increases family peace on every other day of the week.

For young children, however, calendaring can be the least engaging activity of the day. To combat this, assign a younger child the job of ensuring that the "family fun" activity or a play-date with a parent is scheduled. Alternatively, consider having small toys or picture books available to quietly occupy the younger children while the bulk of the scheduling is done.

Executive planning: Just like a bishopric needs to meet prior to meeting with the ward council, a husband and wife need time together to coordinate, express love, and review their underlying goals. Getting on the same page as a couple, at least once a week, can bring your family leadership up a level.

46

INDIVIDUAL INTERVIEWS

(ages 3 and up)

Main Idea: Take time on the Sabbath to counsel with each of your children.

The Details: Sunday is a perfect time for one-on-one time with your children. Some families have both parents present for the interview. Other families have one parent present. Whether it is a formal or casual visit, it is a time to express love and to give and receive counsel.

Elder Ballard taught, "In these last days it is essential—even critical—that parents and children listen to and learn from one another" ("Mothers and Daughters," *Ensign,* May 2010).

You may choose to make interviews a fast Sunday tradition or have them take place more frequently. There is no one right way to do them, but it *is* right to do them. One father chose the weekly option. Every Sunday he met with each child to address the principle in Luke 2:52: "And Jesus increased in wisdom and stature, and in favour with God and man." This father ensured that each child had ongoing goals in those four areas and felt that this one Sunday tradition had blessed his family immensely.

Seasoned parents advise that the most important part of these interviews is to be quiet and listen without interrupting. Often children benefit more from a listening ear than quick counsel.

When you do want to inquire further, here are a few possible questions to ask:

- What things are going well for you?
- Tell me what you have been doing in Duty to God/Personal Progress/Faith in God? What goals are you working on?
- What are the challenges you face?

- What are good things/hard things going on with your friends?
- Tell me about your relationship with your siblings?
- How are your prayers and scripture study?
- What is the best thing in your life now?
- How is your relationship with Mom? With Dad?
- Is there anything you are concerned about?
- What can we do to be better parents?
- What would you like to do for family fun?

Invite each child to individually meet with parents. Shower children with heartfelt love and meaningful praise during your visit. And remember to really listen.

Tip: If possible, start interviewing children when they are young. This establishes a strong habit that proves helpful when older children may be less enthusiastic about the idea.

Part 5

SPECIAL GUESTS AND FIELD TRIPS

OCCASIONALLY, WE GET A LITTLE stir-crazy on Sundays since we try to avoid a few of the activities we normally do during the week. We have found that now and then it is helpful to have a meaningful field trip or Sunday-appropriate outing. It can be refreshing to have a change of scenery and a different teaching venue.

Another way to add variety to your Sunday is to invite people to come and visit. One of our neighbors uses Sunday as a day to reach out to people who have not been coming to church or haven't yet been baptized. You may choose to invite a ward member or family over so you can all get to know each other better.

For some people (like me!), the idea of cooking a fancy meal for others and feeling the need to have a perfect house and well-behaved children may seem overwhelming. So, keep things simple. I've found that sharing a "Sunday snack" with a visitor is as good as or better than sharing a meal! Remind yourself that the goodwill and love generated by inviting somebody over for a visit far overshadows the cleanliness of the house or the quality of the food.

47

RETURNED MISSIONARY GUESTS

Main Idea: Invite recently returned missionaries to come to your home to share their missionary experiences.

The Details: Frequently when a young man or woman in our ward comes home from a mission, we invite him or her to our home to tell our children about their missionary service. They may bring pictures, tell stories, and teach our children a principle of the gospel. Some might even bring visuals from the country where they served!

If you live in a ward without many missionaries, tap into the missionaries who have served from your stake. The high council hears a report from each returning missionary so they might be able to help you contact those who have returned.

Having returned missionaries come and speak to your family is simple and inspiring. The returned missionaries love having a fresh audience. Feeling their enthusiasm and excitement can help your family members catch fire with the gospel too. While we sometimes have them for dinner, we've found they are equally happy if we share treats instead. (We're always trying to keep things simple!)

Call a returned missionary today and invite them to your home to tell your family about his or her mission this coming Sunday. Both the missionary and your family will be blessed and edified. And don't forget to ask questions about wild animals!

Personal note: The returned missionaries usually ask our children if they have any questions. One question our kids love to ask is what experiences the missionaries had with animals on their mission. We've heard stories of being chased by dogs, incidents with armadillos, spiders the size of your hand, eating bugs, and many, many more. I asked one of my sons what he likes best about having the returned missionaries tell us about their missions, and he said, "Definitely the stories about the wild animals!" Whatever it takes!

Tip: Your returned missionary guest does not have to be a recently returned missionary. If you live in an area with few currently returning missionaries, invite others who may have returned years ago but still have inspiring stories to share.

48

WISDOM FROM NEAR AND FAR

Main Idea: Similar to the previous chapter on "Returned Missionary Guests," the purpose of this activity is to tap into others' experiences and testimonies to fortify your family and bring the Spirit of the Lord into your home. Such sharing often strengthens relationships within the family and with other ward members or neighbors with whom you might otherwise interact only superficially. Even though parents are their children's best teachers, it can be beneficial to let people outside of your immediate family be powerful second witnesses.

The Details: Invite family, neighbors, ward members, and youth to your home. Consider asking visitors to share a time when they felt the hand of the Lord in their life, when a scripture gave them needed direction, when they felt an answer to a prayer, when they felt the influence or companionship of the Holy Ghost, or when they felt blessed for following the prophet. Some visitors will prefer to share one experience; others may prefer to talk more.

There are many ways to implement this idea. Consider the following suggestions:

- When family visits or you visit family, invite them to share uplifting, testimony-building experiences.

- Older members of the ward often love to share their wisdom. Invite them over and tell them you just want to get to know them and learn from their experiences.

- Invite youth into your home in pairs or small groups, which may help them feel more comfortable. With the *Come Follow Me* curriculum, which gives youth opportunities to teach and testify, it may be appropriate to invite the youth to come prepared to share a spiritual experience, their favorite scripture, something they are learning in seminary, or a time when they were guided by the Spirit. Sunday is a family day for them too, so you may not want to have youth over regularly, or for a lengthy amount of time, but now and then it can be a blessing to your family and the youth involved.

- Think of someone who you would like to get to know better and to strengthen or be strengthened by. Give them a call and invite them over for this Sunday. Propose a tradeoff: treats from you in exchange for the sharing of an experience or two from them.

The Spirit of the Lord is present and sweet when tender and heartfelt experiences are shared, even in an informal setting over Sunday snacks. These may be some of your favorite Sunday moments.

49

PLAN OF SALVATION FIELD TRIPS

Main Idea: Reflect on the "big picture" of God's plan by going to nearby places that are relevant to the doctrine of the Plan of Salvation—where we came from, why we are here, and where we are going.

At the beginning of each year, no matter which book of scripture is studied in seminary, the curriculum requires the first few lessons be focused on the Plan of Salvation. Reviewing this doctrine is so important that it is done at the start of each seminary year, for four straight years! It is knowledge of the Plan of Salvation that provides the necessary foundation for the doctrine and scriptures taught.

The Details: Plan of Salvation field trips entail going to any place that has relevance to a part of the Plan, then connecting the place with the particular principles.

The following are a few examples of places to visit:

- Visit a cemetery. Even if one of your ancestors was not buried at the cemetery nearest you, go to the cemetery and talk about how death is a part of God's plan.

- Visit a hospital or visit a newborn. This is a great venue for talking about birth as a part of the Plan and how we left a heavenly home to have experiences on earth without the memory of heaven. Read Jeremiah 1:5 to generate a discussion about how our Heavenly Father knew us before we were born.

- Go to a garden or arboretum near your home to reflect on the Creation and the purpose of this earth's creation. A peaceful outdoor garden could welcome a discussion on the significant events that occurred in the Garden of Eden, the Garden of Gethsemane, and the Sacred Grove, as well as their purpose in the Plan.

- Visit a courthouse, jail, or police station to teach that there are consequences of our actions. Although a courthouse might be closed on Sunday, just sitting outside and talking about what happens in the building can be effective. The same is true for a police station. You may see an officer who will be willing to talk to your children for a few minutes about choices and consequences, providing family members with a new perspective.

- Go to the sacrament preparation room or sacrament table to reflect again on the sacrament and the blessings of the Atonement. You might have the building to yourself as you talk about the Last Supper, the institution of the sacrament, and the purpose of this holy ordinance.

50

I LOVE TO SEE THE TEMPLE

Main Idea: Just walking on temple grounds, being near the temple, and touching the temple invites the Spirit of the Lord. President Monson has said: "As we touch the temple and love the temple, our lives will reflect our faith" ("Blessings of the Temple," *Ensign*, October 2010).

In preparation for a special speech, the Nephites gathered together, "every man having his tent with the door thereof towards the temple" (Mosiah 2:6). Elder Gary E. Stevenson stated: "Understanding the eternal nature of the temple will draw you to your family; understanding the eternal nature of the family will draw you to the temple" ("Sacred Homes, Sacred Temples," *Ensign*, May 2009).

Surprise your family with an outing to the temple. Walk the grounds together and feel the Spirit of the Lord.

The Details: A visit to the temple on a Sunday afternoon can remind family members of the majesty and power of the Lord's house and of the significance of the covenants we make there. Gazing at the temple, feeling the peace of the surroundings, you and your children can talk about the blessings the family has received from covenants made in this sacred building.

President Boyd K. Packer counseled: "Say the word *temple*. Say it quietly and reverently. Say it over and over again. *Temple. Temple. Temple.* Add the word *holy. Holy Temple.* Say it as though it were capitalized, no matter where it appears in the sentence.

"Temple. One other word is equal in importance to a Latter-day Saint. *Home.* Put the words *holy temple* and *home* together, and you have described the house of the Lord!" ("The Temple, the Priesthood," *Ensign*, May 1993).

You may choose to make this field trip on a Sunday near your wedding anniversary or your ancestors' wedding anniversary. The importance of marriage in the Plan of Salvation, in the context of linking our families together, becomes even more paramount.

Depending on the ages of your children, you may bring talks on the temple, scriptures, and journals—or just be together as you feel and appreciate the spirit of the temple. Pray for the Spirit of the Lord to be with you and your family as you travel to the nearest temple together and walk the grounds. Invite family members to pray as well.

51

VISIT THE WIDOWS AND THE FATHERLESS

Main Idea: Take some time on Sunday to bring cheer and aid to those whom the Savior would likely visit first if He were in your area.

The Details: Identify people who live nearby whom you could visit. For better or for worse, there are plenty of options for this activity. No matter what state or country we have lived in through the years, our neighborhoods and wards have overflowed with widows, widowers, single sisters or brothers, and children who, for whatever reason, are without a present parent. Call up a neighbor or ward member who falls under the general umbrella of "widow or fatherless." Find out what kind of visit or service they would like, and do it!

This activity requires flexibility because each person found in the category of "widow and fatherless" has different needs. Some people might appreciate a surprise drop-by visit, while others prefer to be forewarned. Some people love to play games and talk for hours, while others wish for only short interactions. Bringing the whole family can make one person rejoice while another really prefers just one or two visitors at a time. Even considering the different needs, we don't need to make this more complicated than it is. The scriptures say to visit the widow and the fatherless and to oppress them not (see Zechariah 7:10). The better we come to know these good people, the better we can do this.

Tip: For those who prefer visiting to playing games, it may be wise to prepare your children on what to talk about during the visit. The questions used for the "Family History Live Recordings" chapter would work well. You may also think of your own questions ahead of time. Possibly include: What memories do you have of when you were our children's age? Tell us about a time when you felt God's love. What was a favorite

Christmas? What advice do you have for us, for our children? What did you like about high school or college? What are some lessons you have learned that you want to pass on?

Personal Note: I don't know what your experience will be, but my perspectives have changed as we have done this activity. For example, I was shocked at the energy of an eighty-three-year-old widow in our ward and was amazed that she could keep up playing games with the five energetic children I brought to her home. Jokes and fun humor filled her house as we all got to know her in a new light.

52

SUNDAY SERVICE

Main Idea: We will be pleased if we retire Sunday evening knowing we have helped someone in need. Elder David L. Beck encouraged: "Minister every day. Opportunities are all around you. Look for them. Ask the Lord to help you recognize them. . . . As you strive to be worthy of the Spirit, you will recognize thoughts and feelings prompting you to minister. As you act on these promptings, you will receive more of them and your opportunities and ability to minister will increase and expand" ("Your Sacred Duty to Minister," *Ensign*, April 2013).

The Details: Sunday service can be as simple as writing letters to missionaries or as involved as making dinner for someone. It can be something that blesses your own family or has you reaching outside of your home. Some ideas include:

- Write letters to the missionaries in your ward or stake. Encourage them and include your favorite uplifting scriptures.

- Make treats for a neighbor, Primary teacher, or ward leader. It may be someone deserving of thanks, love, or friendship. Deliver the treats with a loving note and scripture.

- Make dinner for a grandparent or someone in need. Involve your family in the cooking and delivering.

- Do a service project for a church of a different denomination in your area.

- Write letters or emails to grandparents or family members who live far away.

- Have your family visit with a ward leader to find the needs of people in your area and do something for one of them.

- Write thank-you notes to ward leaders, school teachers, or others who bless you in large and small ways.

- Assign Secret Service Pals (SSP) within the family and allow time for each person to do a secret service for their SSP. Write the names of each family member on separate pieces of paper and place them in a bowl. Then each family member draws a name out of the bowl, redrawing if you happen to pick your own. The name drawn out of the bowl then becomes the family member for whom you do secret service. If you choose to make his bed, or write a love note, sign the note "from your SSP." These secret acts bring the Spirit of the Lord to your home. Some families continue the SSP assignments for the entire week.

Decide what Sunday service you will do. Don't let anything stop you from doing as the Savior did. As the hymn states, "Go and do something today!" ("Have I Done Any Good?" *Hymns*, no. 223) You will be following the Savior's example. When the Pharisees criticized Him for healing on the Sabbath, Jesus replied, "It is lawful to do well on the sabbath days" (see Matthew 12:10–13).

CONCLUSION

I AM AN IMPERFECT PARENT and I have imperfect children. If my family can be blessed by these activities, so can yours. Elder L. Tom Perry admonished, "Let your family be filled with love as you honor the Sabbath all day long and experience its spiritual blessings throughout the week. . . . Let us prepare and conduct ourselves on the Sabbath in a manner that will call down the blessings promised us upon ourselves and our families" ("The Sabbath and the Sacrament," *Ensign*, May 2011). We *can* conduct ourselves on the Sabbath in such a way "that will call down the blessings promised us." We can do it!

For years I have tried to make our Sabbaths more meaningful. Even with many successes and Spirit-filled Sabbaths, I still often become discouraged. Since I already feel swamped, it can seem daunting to think that I need to add an additional item on my "to do" list, particularly on a day of rest. I have found encouragement and hope in what President Eyring taught: "My experience has taught me this about how people and organizations improve: the best place to look is for *small changes* we could make in things we do often. There is power in steadiness and repetition" ("The Lord Will Multiply the Harvest," *An Evening with Elder Henry B. Eyring*, Address given to the Church Educational System, February 6, 1998; emphasis added).

This counsel makes me want to rejoice! To make the greatest impact, I just need to make *small* changes in what I am already doing. Regarding the Sabbath, this may mean using mealtime (since we are already having meals) to talk about what everyone learned at church. It may possibly include reserving a child's favorite cereal for Sunday to put him in a happy mood. Another small change could involve altering Sunday meals to make them meaningful, or simplifying them to allow more time and energy for other activities.

Making a small change might include blocking out thirty minutes every Sunday for family gospel study time. It may look like finding a time my family is already assembled, then sharing a story of Jesus and allowing time for everyone to write in their journals. It could mean choosing one gospel-centered activity to enjoy before Sunday dinner.

I hope you will find strength in and delight in the Sabbath. Your catalyst will be faith in the Lord and your motivation will be to honor Him and His holy day. I wholeheartedly agree with what Elder Russell M. Nelson taught: "Faith in God engenders a love for the Sabbath; faith in the Sabbath engenders a love for God. A sacred Sabbath truly is a delight" ("The Sabbath Is a Delight," *Ensign,* May 2015).

The Sabbath is made for man (see Mark 2:27). It is a day set apart—a day to rest from our labors and to pay our devotions to God. Thankfully, it is a day to enjoy family togetherness, to deepen our testimonies, and to increase gospel knowledge. Truly there is a power in the Holy Sabbath that can strengthen you and fortify your family.

As we have tried to make our Sunday activities more purposeful, we have felt an increase of love, joy, and contentment. Our thoughts are elevated. Our ability to always remember the Savior is increased. Personal revelation flows. Life is found in greater abundance. This is the joy of the gospel. This is the power of the Sabbath.

Appendix A
ACTIVITIES BY AGE

NOTE: OFTEN THERE IS OVERLAP in the age groupings since most of the activities are designed to span multiple age groups.

Ideal for ages 3–6

- Gospel Games (Part 1): Scripture Land (chapter 1); Reverse Gospel Pictionary (chapter 2); Chutes and Ladders—Scripture Style (chapter 3); Sunday Charades (chapter 4); Apples to Chapels (chapter 5); Gospel 20 Questions (chapter 6); Bible Balderdash (chapter 7—drawing images); The Magic Sunday Square (chapter 11); Scripture Basketball (chapter 12).

- Significant Dates/Anniversary Celebrations (Part 2): Young children will love *simple* celebrations for *all* these dates; they will especially love learning from the gospel art pictures that go with the events.

- Family History Snowballing (Part 3): Sharing Mission Record (chapter 28); Joy in Past Journeys (chapter 29); Focus on Faces, levels one and two (chapter 30); Ancestor Anniversaries and Birthdays (chapter 31); Grandparent Guesstures (chapter 32); When I Was Young (chapter 33).

- Gospel Study (Part 4): Explore the Sources (chapter 36); Miraculous Music (chapter 38), Amazing Memorizing (chapter 41); Gospel Art (chapter 42); Power from the Prophets (chapter 43); Family Council without the Family Feud (chapter 45), and Individual Interviews (chapter 46).

- Special Guests and Field Trips (Part 5): the visits, guests, and trips may be meaningful for some children this age. In particular, young children will enjoy I Love to See the Temple (chapter 50) and Sunday Service (chapter 52).

- In addition, you may want to create some sort of Sunday Treasure Box that has items the children can use only on Sunday: playdough; paint; certain puzzles, toys, or books that can bring newness and uniqueness to the day.

Ideal for ages 7–11

ALL ideas contained in this book are great for this age group—enjoy this stage of eager learning and have high expectations of their capabilities!

Ideal for ages 12–122

All ideas are appropriate, except possibly Scripture Land and Chutes and Ladders—Scripture Style. If poor attitudes or non-compliance become a challenge at this stage, the following suggestions may be beneficial:

- Separate the older children from the younger children. Give the older children a challenging activity or task to accomplish on their own while you focus on the younger children.

- Offer simple rewards for those who participate politely.

- Try two approaches at different times: first, allow as much freedom as possible by letting them choose which activity goes on which Sunday of the month (for the Sabbath System plan) or which activity they would like to do that day; second, give specific direction suited to their capabilities, like inviting them to prepare a lesson on the Word of Wisdom from *True to the Faith*, or report on a section from *Preach My Gospel.*

- Capitalize on the ideas that also meet the person's interests: **Food** is made meaningful with the suggestions in the Significant Dates section and Ancestor Birthdays chapter. **Competition** can be used with the Family History Snowballing section, Magic Sunday Square (chapter 11), and Scripture Sports (chapter 12). **Other people** may offer unique perspectives, and teens are more likely to lend an ear to someone new (see Special Guests section). **Rewards** motivate activities in the Gospel Study section; and **Pure Fun** is a motivator for Gospel Games.

Remember that even though there might be resistance, often the desire to participate is present, just hidden. Initiate the game or activity and they will likely come and participate.

Appendix B
A SYSTEM FOR YOUR SABBATH

TRULY THE SABBATH DAY CAN be a delight with some effort. Waking up Sunday morning with a system in place will help things run smoothly. Just as it is much easier for a substitute teacher to come in and effectively teach if there is a plan in place, it is easier for a tired, busy parent to lead the family in worshipful activities if there is already a system set up. A structure simply makes the ideal more likely to happen.

You may want to be strategic in choosing which activity to do on specific Sundays of the month. For example, on fast Sunday your emotional tolerance and patience levels may be lower, so choose activities accordingly. Perhaps responsibilities with your current ward calling might be heavier on a certain week and may impact the type of activities you implement. Some ideas may not be well-suited for the current stage of your family; modify your plan to meet your own needs.

A Sabbath System is just one way for possible planning but is, of course, not the only way. Just as the Sabbath was made for man and not man for the Sabbath, remember the Sabbath System is made for man and not man for the Sabbath System. In other words, the Sabbath System is there to simplify, not to cause unnecessary stress on a day that should be set apart from other busy days. It must ultimately allow for flexibility. Always, the emphasis should not be on accomplishing certain prescribed activities, as worthwhile as they may be, but on assisting family members to remember the Savior, feel the joy of His gospel, and look forward to His holy day.

Three Steps for Creating Your Sabbath System

First, choose the time of the day and amount of time you want to engage in meaningful activities as a family. Maybe you want to have a Power

Hour and have four, fifteen-minute activities (or Power Half-Hour with two activities). You may decide to gather right after dinner, or first thing in the morning after everyone is dressed for church. The time you choose will likely change from year to year, based on your ward meeting time and the changing needs of your family.

Second, choose the overarching goal. Maybe you want to have a focus theme of the month or have activities from a certain section only one Sunday of the month. It may be helpful to involve your children in this step.

Third, choose your favorite activities and plan when you will do them. This includes deciding which month or which Sundays to do your selected activities.

Create your own Sabbath System by filling in the blanks below

Time of day: _____ Duration: _____

Overarching Goal: _____

Specific activities: _____

First Sunday of the month: _____

Second Sunday of the month: _____

Third Sunday of the month: _____

Fourth Sunday of the month: _____

Below are two examples of Sabbath Systems. Consider tailoring one of them to meet your family's needs.

Sample Sabbath System 1

Focus on one theme for the entire month

You may decide to focus on one area for a whole month and then rotate to a new area the next month. For example, Family History Snowballing the first month, Gospel Games the next month, Gospel Study the following month. Below is a sample Sabbath System for a month with the focus on Family History Snowballing. A month of Gospel Games or Gospel Study would follow a similar format. The system below includes two ideas a week but you may prefer to do a different amount.

Time: Each Sunday we will meet together for one hour (e.g. 10 a.m.–11 a.m.)

Goal: We want to focus on one theme for the month and choose activities from that theme each Sunday.

Plan:

- First Sunday of the month: one or two of your choice, perhaps "Indexing Races" (chapter 26) and/or "Family History Quiz Creations" (chapter 27).
- Second Sunday of the month: perhaps "Sharing Mission Records" (chapter 28) and/or "Joy in Past Journeys" (chapter 29).
- Third Sunday of the month: perhaps "Focus on Faces" (chapter 30) and/or "Grandparent Guesstures" (chapter 32).
- Fourth Sunday of the month: perhaps "When I Was Young" (chapter 33) and/or "Jump to Journaling" (chapter 35).
- Fifth Sunday (if one falls this month): "Family History Live Recordings" (chapter 34). and/or "Ancestor Anniversaries and Birthdays" (chapter 31).

Sample Sabbath System #2

Weekly activities are rotated from different themes

Time: Every Sunday we will spend one hour (e.g. between 2:00–3:00 p.m.) in family time.

Goal: During this time, we plan to have a family council and discuss what we learned in church. We also want to do two additional activities that will change, based on the structure below.

Plan:

- First Sunday of the month—"Stories of Jesus" (chapter 44), "Individual Interviews" (chapter 46).
- Second Sunday of the month—Two ideas from Gospel Games that rotate each month: "Bible Balderdash" (chapter 7) and "Gospel 20 Questions" (chapter 6).
- Third Sunday of the month—Two ideas from Family History Snowballing that rotate each month: "When I Was Young" (chapter 33) and "Focus on Faces" (chapter 30).

- Fourth Sunday of the month—Two ideas from Gospel Study that rotate each month: "Amazing Memorizing" (chapter 41) and "Explore the Sources" (chapter 36).

For the months that follow, we plan to substitute new activities following the pattern above. In addition, we may occasionally have a special guest or field trip. On Sundays that fall on significant dates or anniversary celebrations, we can focus the teaching around that theme (see Part 2).

In the second Sabbath System above, the family wanted to place an emphasis on "Stories of Jesus" and have once-a-month interviews, so they kept those on the first week of every month. Another family may choose to study *Preach My Gospel* every week. Still another family may feel that it is important to have a gospel game and a gospel study activity each week. Feel free to be as random, purposeful, or creative as you desire when designing your own Sabbath System.

ACKNOWLEDGMENTS

FIRST AND FOREMOST, I WOULD you like to thank my parents for their fervent testimony of the Sabbath day. They teach by their words and example of the great good that can happen on the Lord's holy day. I also thank my husband, John Hilton III, for encouraging me to record my ideas, keeping the home running smoothly while I wrote, and providing valuable insights. Thank you to my children, Levi, Annemarie, Maria, Joseph, Katrina, and Rebekah, who are a treasure to their parent and who are fairly patient with me when I don't do it all. Thanks to Lisa Roper for her professional insights in the initial stages of the manuscript and to Samantha Millburn, Shauna Humphreys, and Kathy Gordon at Covenant for their honest feedback, clever ideas, and professional edits. Thank you to Michelle Pipitone for the cover design and layout. And thank you to Stephanie Lacey for marketing my book.

The following people read drafts and offered helpful suggestions: Emily Baird, Jill Judd, Janet Hales, Klea Harris, Ann Henstrom, Shawna Hilton, Erin Holmes, Heather Moore, Adam Miller, Heather Spears Olsen, Lori Olsen, Mindy Olsen, Sally Olsen, Sarah Olsen, Moe Peck, Lise Powell, Robin Richards, Janet Salls, Ashley Speirs, Rebecca Tayler, Vicky Taylor, and Heidi Tyler. I am very grateful for their insights.

Finally, I am grateful to my Father in Heaven for the strength, clear inspiration, and feeling of excitement I receive as I parent and as I write. I love Him and give Him credit for any good that may come from this book.

ABOUT THE AUTHOR

LANI OLSEN HILTON IS THE coauthor of *What Girls Need to Know About Guys/ What Guys Need to Know About Girls*. She is a frequent speaker at Education Week and Especially for Youth. Lani (rhymes with Bonnie) is the fifth of twelve children and the mother of six. Her parents, Maynard and Sally Olsen, created a home in which making the Sabbath a delight was a high priority. From these Sunday family times, Lani came to love and get excited about the gospel of Jesus Christ. Lani has served as a seminary teacher, Primary chorister, Young Women leader, and Relief Society instructor and loves teaching the gospel to all age groups.